CW00821418

MODEL
SAILING YACHTS

HOW TO BUILD, RIG AND SAIL THEM

(REVISED EDITION)

A PRACTICAL HANDBOOK FOR MODEL YACHTSMEN

EDITED
BY

PERCIVAL MARSHALL, C.I.MECH.E.

Copyright © 2013 Read Books Ltd.
This book is copyright and may not be
reproduced or copied in any way without
the express permission of the publisher in writing

British Library Cataloguing-in-Publication Data
A catalogue record for this book is available from the
British Library

CONTENTS

MODEL BUILDING 1

PREFACE 9

CHAPTER I - INTRODUCTORY 13

CHAPTER II - THE RATING OF
MODEL YACHTS.. 35

CHAPTER III - BUILDING A 36 IN. MODEL
YACHT BY THE CARVEDHULL METHOD............. 49

CHAPTER IV - BUILDING A MODEL
10-RATER 73

CHAPTER V - THE CONSTRUCTION OF
"BUILT-UP" ORPLANKED YACHTS 88

CHAPTER VI - SPARS AND FITTINGS 106

CHAPTER VII - STEERING GEARS 116

CHAPTER VIII - RACING SCHOONERS 123

CHAPTER IX - TUNING UP AND SAILING 139

CHAPTER X - NOTES ON SAILING
FOR BEGINNERS 152

Model Building

Model building as a hobby involves the creation of models either from kits, or from materials and components acquired by the builder. The most common form of modelling is the 'scale model', produced with varying degrees of accuracy, dependent on the interests and intentions of the creator. This is most generally a physical representation of an object, which maintains accurate relationships between all important aspects of the model, although absolute values of the original properties need not be preserved. Scale models are used in many fields including engineering, architecture, film making, military command, salesmanship and most widely, for fun with hobby model building. While each field may use a scale model for a different purpose, all scale models are based on the same principles and must meet the same general requirements to be functional.

Perhaps the most common form of model building is model cars, or toy cars. This category can often include other miniature motor vehicles, such as trucks, buses, or even ATVs as well. Because many miniature vehicles were originally aimed as children as playthings, there is no precise difference between a model car and a toy car, yet the word 'model' implies either assembly required or some attempt at accurate rendering of an actual vehicle at smaller scale. Regarding the former, the kit building hobby became popular through the 1950s, while the collecting of miniatures by adults started to pick up steam around 1970. Precision detailed miniatures made specifically for adults are a significant part of the market since perhaps the mid-1980s

Miniature models of automobiles first appeared about the time real automobiles did - first in Europe and then, shortly after, in the United States. These were initially duplicates made of lead and brass, and later in the twentieth century, made of slush cast plaster or iron. Tin and pressed steel cars, trucks, and military vehicles, like those made by Bing of Germany followed in the 1920s through the 1940s, but models rarely copied actual vehicles - it is unclear why, but likely had to do with the crudeness of early casting and metal shaping techniques which prevented precision rendering of an actual car's shape and detail. Casting vehicles in various alloys, usually zinc (called zamac or mazac), also started during these decades and came on stronger in the late 1930s, prominent particularly after World War II. Today, China, and other countries of Southeast Asia are the main producers of metal miniature vehicles from European, American, and Japanese companies. For the most part, only specialty models for collectors are still made in the Europe or the United States.

Another incredibly popular form of modelling is aircraft; be they models of existing or imaginary aeroplanes. Such models vary enormously in complexity, and can be flying or non-flying (static), and may or may not be an accurate scale model of a full-size design. Flying models range from simple toy gliders made of card stock or foam polystyrene to powered scale models made from materials such as balsa wood or fibreglass. Some can be very large, especially when used to research the flight properties of a proposed real design. The models intended for static display are usually made as highly accurate reproductions, requiring, in some cases hundreds, or even thousands of hours of work. Simpler models, for the amateur modeller are available in kit form however, typically made of injection-moulded polystyrene.

Most of the world's airlines allow their fleet aircraft to be modelled as a form of publicity, and in the early days of air travel, airlines would order large models of their aircraft and supply them to travel agencies as a promotional item. In a very similar way, the shipping industry was one of the first promoters of model ships; model building is a craft as old as shipbuilding itself, stretching back to ancient times when water transport was first developed. Some of the oldest surviving European ship models have been those of early craft such as galleys, galleons, and possibly carracks, dating from the twelfth through to the fifteenth centuries and found occasionally mounted in churches, where they were used in ceremonies to bless ships and those who sailed in them, or as votive offerings for successful voyages or surviving peril at sea, a practice which remained common in Catholic countries until the nineteenth century.

A consequence of Britain's naval supremacy in the eighteenth and nineteenth centuries was wide public interest in ships and ship models. Numerous fairly crude models were built as children's toys leading to the creation of functional, as opposed to decorative, ship models. Britain also led the world in model ship sailing clubs - in 1838 the Serpentine Sailing Society was started in Hyde Park, followed by the first London Model Yacht Club in 1845. By the 1880s there were three model sailing clubs sharing the Kensington Gardens Round Pond alone. Perhaps one of the most popular forms of model ships however, was (and is) the 'ship in a bottle.' The simplest way of constructing this seemingly impossible feat is to rig the masts of the ship and raise it up when the ship is inside the bottle. Masts, spars, and sails are built separately and then attached to the hull of the ship with strings and hinges so the masts can lie flat against the deck. The ship is then placed inside the bottle and the masts are pulled up using the strings attached to the masts. Make sure the hull of the ship still fits through the opening though! Alternatively, with specialized long-handled tools, it is possible to build the ship inside the bottle.

Last but not least, in this brief tour of modern and historical modelling, railway models are an incredibly popular sub-genre; worthy of an entire introduction on their own. The scale models include locomotives, rolling stock, streetcars, tracks, signalling, roads, buildings, vehicles, model figures, lights, and features such as streams, hills and canyons. The earliest model railways were the 'carpet railways' in the 1840s. Electric trains appeared around the start of the twentieth century, but these were crude likenesses compared with the model trains of today. Now, modellers (hobbyists and professionals) create modern railway and road layouts, often recreating real locations and periods in history.

Involvement ranges from possession of a train set, to spending hours and large sums on an enormous and exacting model of a railroad and the scenery through which it passes, called a 'layout'. These range in size, with some large enough to ride. For many people who build railway models, the eventual goal is to eventually run the layout as if it were a real railroad (if the layout is based on the fancy of the builder) or as the real railroad did (if the layout is based on a prototype). If modellers choose to model a prototype, they may reproduce track-by-track reproductions of the real railroad in miniature, often using prototype track diagrams and historic maps. Probably the largest model landscape in the UK is in the Pendon Museum in Oxfordshire, UK, where a 1:76.2 scale model of the Vale of White Horse in the 1930s is under construction. The museum also houses one of the earliest scenic models - the Madder Valley layout built by John Ahern. The largest live steam layout, with 25 miles (40 km) of track is Train Mountain in Chiloquin, Oregon, U.S.

The Schooner "Prospero."
Close hauled on starboard tack

PREFACE

THERE are two distinct types of model yachtsmen: firstly, the man who admires a model yacht for her good general qualities and sails her for the love of the sport, and secondly, the racing enthusiast with whom speed is a primary consideration. The former can get his pleasure alone if he wishes; he will be happy with his boat. The latter must find other boats to race against, and must join a sailing club so that he may give play to his sporting instincts in club and inter-club regattas. This book should be useful to both classes of model yachtsmen, though naturally the racing enthusiast will need to pursue his studies more deeply than these pages provide for, if he is to achieve premier honours. He will, however, gain much useful knowledge in friendly intercourse with his fellow club-members, and will learn much from his experiences in racing. Model yachtsmen generally are friendly folk, only too willing to impart their knowledge to the novice, and to encourage him along the road to success.

This handbook, first published many years ago, has earned a very favourable reputation as a reliable introduction to serious model yachting. The present edition has been revised and brought thoroughly up to date, particularly in the matter of rating rules and modern designs. A new chapter has been added, giving a design and instructions for building a 36 in. model yacht, suitable for a beginner. We have to acknowledge the friendly help of several leaders in the model yachting world, and especially of the late Mr. C. N. Forge, Mr. W. J. E. Pike (Hon. Secretary of the Model Yachting Association), and Mr. R. H. Morrell.

MODEL SAILING YACHTS

CHAPTER I

INTRODUCTORY

MODEL YACHTING, as a scientific and fascinating sport for both the young and those of mature years, has now obtained that recognition which it deserves. During the last fifty years it has been modestly followed by many people, but in more recent times it has made such strides that, instead of being classed as child's play, it has now engaged the serious attention of the sport-loving public, and the circle of its votaries widens as its delights as a pastime and the practical lessons to be derived from it, when intelligently pursued, become more and more known.

The practical model yachtsman is, as often as not, a "landsman" with very indistinct notions as to the merits of the different types of yachts or the meaning of the various nautical terms used. However, the experience which can only be gained by practice, together with the knowledge to be obtained from the careful study of this book, will soon enable the novice to enjoy the pastime.

There is, of course, as much difference between the scale

model yacht designed and built by the professional or skilled amateur as there is between the shilling tin toy engine and a scale model locomotive. The novice is often at a loss to know why the gorgeously painted toy, newly purchased in the bazaar, lies flat down on its side directly it is placed in the water and refuses to right itself, notwithstanding the assurance of the salesman that it is a perfect model of the latest most successful large yacht; whilst the little simple looking schooner scarcely half its size and obviously homemade, belonging to the mechanic on the other side of the pond, is slipping along and increasing her speed as she gracefully heels to each puff of wind. Again, the novice does not understand why it is that the splendid model of a full rigged frigate, with complete equipment of brass anchors and rows of cannon tastefully arranged along her deck, insists upon sailing backwards or continues slowly to turn round like a top as she drifts from one end of the pond to the other, and yet that simple jib and mainsail rigged boat with her racing flag at the masthead seems to be sailing straight against the wind, increasing her speed the harder it blows.

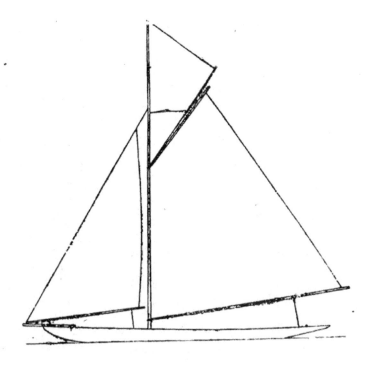

Fig. 1.—Sloop rig

Model yacht sailing does not consist of merely placing your boat in the water and waiting to see where she will go. However perfect a model may be, unless she is handled by a yachtsman who has a fair knowledge of the principles of sailing she may be badly beaten, both for speed and direction, by an inferior boat. He who has a knowledge of the correct way to sail a boat, and the principles of design and construction employed in building her, can set his model yacht on a given course and know just what she will do under certain conditions of wind.

Fig. 2.—Cutter rig

The sport of model yachting should appeal strongly to us, a maritime people. Its great fascination lies in there being no finality in it; it is an art, not an exact science; sufficient can be positively stated as to cause and effect to give confidence, and the interest is maintained in the following up of all the elusive factors which are called in being. As a pastime it would be very hard to beat, as, firstly, the designing and building may occupy its followers in the drawing-room and workshop during the dark winter evenings, and the finished models provide healthy and pleasant recreation in the open air in the summer.

Types of Yachts

Although the evolution in the type of yacht hulls is greatly influenced by the designer's ideas of what is the best form for speed, the performance of any particular hull may largely depend upon the kind of rig and the proportion of area that the various sails bear to each other. The most simple rig of all is the jib and mainsail rig, which consists of the two sails mentioned, only, and is the most popular rig with the racing model yachtsman, on account of the exactness with which the varying angles of the sails with the amidships line of hull found most suitable for certain directions of course and wind can be consistently reproduced, the methods of doing so being explained later in the chapter on sailing. As reefing is hardly practical in a model yacht, it is the custom to have, in the case of this type of sail plan, two or three rigs of different areas, each reduced to scale in correct graduation; and as in most model yacht clubs the members have their sails already fitted on separate spars, it is only the work of a few moments to change from one to the other, according to the amount of sail their model will carry for the strength of wind prevailing.

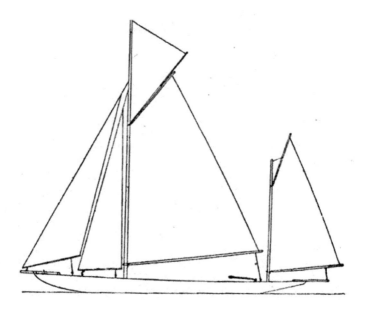

Fig. 3.—Yawl rig

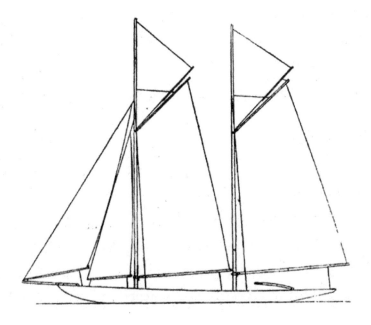

Fig. 4.—Ketch rig

The cutter rig (Fig. 2), which consists of four sails, may be so arranged that the top sail may be either removed altogether or replaced by others of smaller area.

In the case of a large yacht all sails have to be hauled up into position by ropes known as halyards, which must lead down to the deck; but the model yachtsman can dispense with a lot of such gear. Recently a prominent designer, for the first time in large yachts, dispensed with the topsail yard, making the topmast itself sufficiently long to set the sail, a practice which has been in vogue with model yachtsmen for many years.

The type shown in Fig. 1 is commonly regarded as the sloop rig, and differs from a cutter in that she only carries one sail forward of the mast.

The yawl rig is similar to that of the cutter, but has a smaller sail set upon another mast (known as the mizzen) abaft the mainsail, the sheet being led aft to a spar projecting behind the counter. In the case of this rig the main-boom has to be considerably shorter than in the cutter rig, so that it does not foul the mizzen mast when it swings.

The ketch rig differs from the yawl rig inasmuch as the mizzen mast is always placed forward of the rudder post, whereas that of a yawl is always stepped aft of the rudder post.

Perhaps the prettiest rig of all is that of the schooner, shown in the frontispiece, but unless the hull so rigged is of perfect formation it is difficult to get this type of boat to go well to windward.

The ketch also has a much larger mizzen sail than the yawl and generally has a topsail with it.

There are many kinds of other rigs—such as topsail schooners, which have square topsails on the foremast; but none excepting those rigs which have been mentioned are often used for sailing yachts.

The Parts of a Model Yacht

The boat proper is termed the hull, the backbone of which is called the keelson, and the lead, which is attached to the latter in order to give the boat stability and power to resist the heeling moment created by the wind pressure upon the sails, is known as the keel.

The opening in the deck which gives access to the interior is called the hatchway, and it is closed by a cover known as the hatch. The extreme forward end of hull is the stem, and the portions forward and aft of the midships section are respectively known as the fore-body and after-body.

The extremities of a hull, the deck of which is longer than the load water line, are known as the overhangs. The after overhang is sometimes termed the counter stern.

In a built-up model the planking is attached to strips of wood known as ribs or timbers.

The sides which rise above the deck are called bulwarks; the part of the bulwarks crossing the stern is called the tafferel, or taffrail, and is usually pierced with holes to allow water to run off the deck.

FITTINGS OF THE HULL.—The bowsprit is passed through a ring at the top of the stem called a cranch or gammon iron, and its end is secured into a socket or between a pair of uprights called the bowsprit bitts, which are fixed to the deck. Metal bars are frequently fixed a short distance above the deck to take rings attached to the sheets, so that the sails can swing freely from one side of the boat to the other; such a bar is called a horse. Metal eyes are screwed into the sides to take the shrouds, and are called chain plates; the eye in the stem is the bobstay plate. In the stern-post are two eyes called gudgeons, to which the rudder is hooked by means of two hooks called pintles. The bar which is fixed into the top of the rudder is the tiller.

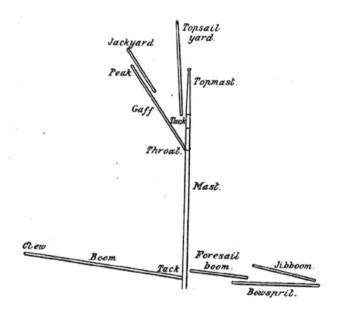

Fig. 5.—Positions and names of spars for a cutter-rigged model yacht

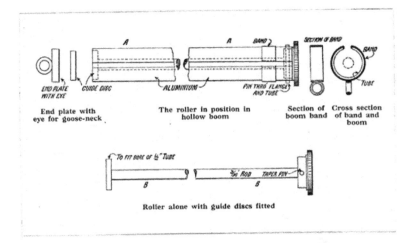

**Fig. 6.—Details showing principle of construction of
Behenna-Langley roller reefing gear for models**

MASTS AND SPARS.—The parts and fittings of a mast
are as follow: The step, the head, the caps, the cross-trees, the
top-mast, the truck, the boom, the gaff; the part which rests
on the mast being called the throat (the sides of which are
the jaws), the end of the gaff is called the peak; the bowsprit
(the end inboard being called the heel), the jib-boom—a term
only used in model yachts, in large vessels the jib-boom is
an extension of the bowsprit—the foresail boom. The small
boom which projects over the stern of a yawl is called the
bumpkin. Spars is a general term which comprises practically
all wooden supports of sails. The spar at the top of a lug-sail
is called the yard: it is distinguished from a boom or gaff by

the fact that it lies against the mast instead of having one end butting on to the mast. Anything belonging to a mainmast should be distinguished by the prefix main—thus mainsail, main boom, main topsail would indicate that they were fixed to the mainmast. In the same way other masts would distinguish their particular fittings, mizzen-sail, fore topmast, etc. The fittings of sails follow the same rule—such as topsail yard, mainsail gaff.

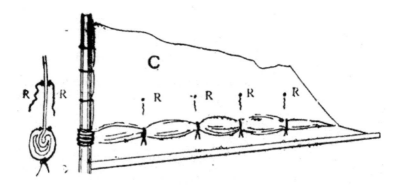

Fig. 7.—Reefing a mainsail

RIGGING.—The bowsprit and masts are, when necessary, supported by ropes stretched tightly to some point of convenient attachment to the hull. The following are those most frequently used on model yachts—topmast stay, bobstay, topmast shrouds, forestay. The rope which is stretched between the masts of a schooner at the tops is called the triatic stay. The bowsprit is sometimes stayed with a rope each side called bowsprit shrouds.

The sails are pulled up and fastened by ropes termed halyards, which are fastened to the upper part of the sail, and are named according to the sail to which they are attached. The jib and foresail each have a halyard attached to their upper corner, and they are called the jib and foresail halyard, respectively. A mainsail carried by a gaff would have two— viz., the throat and peak halyards, because they lift the throat and peak of the sail. The amount of movement of the sails and, therefore, the angle which they make with the centre line of the boat, is controlled by ropes called sheets, and which take their names from the sail which they control, such as the main sheet, the jib sheet, the fore sheet, and so on. Readers will take note of this—that the term "sheet" means a rope and not a sail; a yachtsman usually refers to the sails by their names, or as "the canvas"

EXTRA SAILS.—In addition to the principal sails of a model yacht, special sails are carried in light winds. The jib topsail is a small light sail used for reaching. The balloon jib is a large light jib hoisted in very weak winds; the spinnaker is used exclusively for sailing with the wind directly astern; the mainsail projecting at right angles out at the other side.

SAILS FOR ROUGH WEATHER.—Mainsails, jibs, and foresails of smaller size are set in place of the fine weather sails, and topsails are taken down altogether or replaced by small ones called jib-headed topsails. If the wind is very rough indeed the mainsail is taken in and replaced by a sail known as a storm trysail; another method of reducing sail is that known as reefing. It consists in rolling up the lower edge or foot of the sail so as to reduce the surface exposed to the wind. The rolled portion is tied up by means of a number of small ropes, R.R., fixed in the sail, or a row of eyelets, and the sail is laced through them. These are called reef points, but, as has before been mentioned, it is better to have separate rigs made to a smaller scale than the largest suit, as the roll of cloth upon the mainboom when reefed often gets wet and heavy, and hampers the boat's performance. Some quite successful mechanical reefing gears have been made. We illustrate the Behenna-Langley gear, which functions by rolling the sail round a hollow boom.

How to Choose a Model Yacht

The reasons which have caused various types of rigs to be adopted in large yachts only partly hold good in respect to model yachts. The questions of handiness in a seaway, the number of men required to handle a given rig, and so on, obviously disappear, and model yacht designers and owners can neglect considerations which would be serious matters in a big yacht. If the model yachtsman intends to make racing and prize-winning his object, then he must select the most speedy and up-to-date design which his pocket can afford, but he should also consider the peculiarities of the water in which most of his racing will be accomplished, and the regulations of the sailing club concerned. Some boats have their best speed and sailing qualities when sailing against the wind, others when the wind is at one side, or "abeam" as the nautical term is. Another type of boat sails very fast before the wind—that is, when it is blowing directly behind her—but may be perhaps slow or uncertain against a wind. Obviously, if the pond is so situated that the prevailing winds will be abeam of the yachts when sailing over the regular course, a yacht should be chosen which sails fast under this condition; but sometimes clubs race against other clubs, and it is far better to have an all-round boat, as the conditions prevailing upon the other waters may differ. It must not be thought that features which make a yacht good on one point of sailing are detrimental to performance on any other point. It was an old idea that this was so, but any model that will go well to windward (which point of sailing is always the first consideration) can easily be made to run and reach well with the present-day steering gear, which is dealt with in a later chapter.

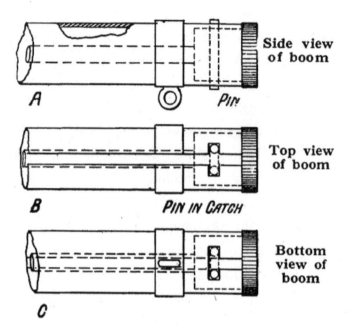

Side view
of boom

A   *PIN*

Top view
of boom

B   *PIN IN CATCH*

Bottom
view of
boom

C

Fig. 8.—Details of Behenna-Langley reefing gear

It does not matter if the boat is of extreme design so long as she conforms to the laws of yacht architecture, which laws determine whether the yacht is capable of being balanced or not. An old saying is "slow and sure," but the harmony of fore-body and after-body and under-water-body to topsides is a harmony which, comprising both speed and steadiness, shows clearly that you must have both or neither. The design for 10-rater *XPDNC* is, for her waterline length, perhaps the most extreme design that can be put down, whilst still retaining the harmony of the whole.

If the reader purchases his yacht, he will do well to make sure that she has a reputation for steady sailing. Whatever he does, the tyro will have to gain his experience by degrees. He will soon find when he commences to sail against expert racing yachtsmen that even with his latest speed marvel his chance of success will be very small at the outset if he sails his boat unaided (and that is where the real pleasure lies). If his yacht sails true he will not have to combat the tricks of an untried or a freak boat, and will soon find that the yacht can be relied on to sail a given course correctly. With the knowledge gained by failures, the intelligent novice soon becomes a serious competitor; an occasional second or third prize may fall to him, and bring further encouragement.

Fig. 9.—A 10-rater in her element

Though racing is very popular, and almost every model yachtsman likes to try conclusions with another boat at some time or other, there is a great deal of fun and pleasure to be obtained from cruising either alone or in company. It is pleasant to watch a model scudding before a light wind on a sunny day with spinnaker set, or on some rough winter day when there is a roaring breeze to see her thrash off a lee shore with storm jib and trysail set. If this part of the sport has greater attractions, then choose a cruising model which has a picturesque appearance (of course, she should have good sailing qualities). She may have a few smart fittings, such as imitation tiller and cabin tops, and yet sail well; a gold line or beading round the side makes a good show, one or two model pulley blocks, or anything of that nature which takes the owner's fancy, so long as it is not overdone. A cutter always looks graceful, but the fore and aft schooner rig is, perhaps, the prettiest of all, and as it has a comparatively large number of sails, provides amusement in setting and changing them. The lateen rig and the gunter lug are also pretty rigs.

As a general rule, the best sailing models are those made by professional model yacht builders, either attached to model yacht clubs or who make a speciality of building high-class models for the trade, and by skilful amateurs. Some of the latter gentlemen turn out work equal to and even superior to the best professional work, so that a good bargain may be obtained occasionally in this way. There are also a number of firms making model work their business who stock very good model yachts, but the general toy shop or bazaar pattern model yacht is not of much use in comparison with the models used by the model yacht clubs. If the yacht is to be sailed in competition with others in a certain club, the best course is to first communicate with the secretary and find out the rule his club has adopted for measuring the boats, so that you may get one which will be eligible and yet not at too great a disadvantage. If you have no particular club in view at the moment, then you can very well go and inspect the stock at one of the model depots, and select one which takes your fancy as something to make a start with. For a good boat you must be prepared to pay a high price—not shillings but pounds; though small models could be bought for under a sovereign, and yet be good sailers in a modest way. These are, however, unsuitable to compete with those used in model yacht races. A first-class model should be equipped with several suits of sails for use in various kinds of weather. The sails should be made of suitable material; those for use in light wind—such as balloon jib, spinnaker, jib topsail, balloon topsail—should be made of very light stuff and be fitted with light spars (cordage must be of water-line and not string). The paint on the hull should be smooth, as a rough surface slows the boat considerably. If you are selecting your boat at a toy shop, pick out one with a heavy lead keel, and, as far as you can judge, one which is well hollowed out inside the hull; prefer rather one which is rigged in a simple style to one which has elaborate fittings and rigging.

Merits of Different Rigs

The best for all-round sailing is the cutter rig, or its modifications—the sloop and Bermudian.

This type of boat is supreme for beating to windward, is fast down wind—that is, scudding—and though inferior to the schooner and lugger when the wind is abeam will sail well with good speed. The yawl is almost as good as the cutter for all-round sailing—that is, the true yawl rig. The yawl rig has been adopted in big yachts to reduce the large mainsail of the cutter rig, and yet retain the power to lie close to the wind when beating to windward; it is more handy, as the boat can be sailed under mizzen and foresail only, when getting into and out of confined places, and fewer men are required to work it. These considerations, of course, do not hold with a model yacht, so that the only justification for its existence is the fancy of the owner, or to enable him to enter his boat in a class which has a rule compelling all yachts to have more than one mast.

The most speedy boats for reaching—that is, with the wind abeam—are schooners and luggers. At this particular point of sailing they will beat a cutter or yawl. The lugger especially is a flier when reaching in a good breeze, and may scud well, but must be very well handled indeed to make a good show when beating to windward. The schooner is almost equal to the lugger when the wind is abeam, is quite as fast down wind and better when beating to windward, though not generally as good to windward as cutter or yawl. Regarding size, this should correspond to the size of the sheet of water in which the model will be sailed. A boat about 2 ft. in length from stem to stern is a very convenient size for small ponds; 2 ft. 6 in. to 3 ft. for medium size ponds; and for lakes or harbours and estuaries, as large as you like up to 6 ft. or so. It is a mistake, in the writer's opinion, to sail large boats upon small ponds. The smallest size which it is advisable to buy is about 30 in. in length over the hull.

When a model yacht is laid up for the winter, or any considerable length of time, it should be unrigged, the spars, sails, and cordage dried and rolled up neatly in calico or paper so as to keep out dust; the hull should also be dried and rubbed over with a rag saturated with linseed or similar oil. It should be covered up and stored in some place free from damp, but yet not in hot air, such as would be the case if put on the top shelf in a room lighted by gas; damp or heat are liable to warp the hull and open the seams.

CHAPTER II

THE RATING OF MODEL YACHTS

A SUITABLE method of measuring the sizes of model yachts for the purpose of racing on level terms has for a long time been the subject of much thought and discussion among model yachtsmen.

Taking a model of a given size it is not difficult to beat her with a larger one even if the latter be of inferior design. It is, therefore, necessary to have some formula by which model yachts may be classed and it is obviously necessary to take such measurements, or to impose such restrictions as will control the sizes of the speed factors. Every model depends upon three of these, and sailing length is the principal one. Sail and the power to carry it more or less upright are the others.

Simplest Method

The simplest method of measuring model yachts is to take the length over all (L.O.A.) and to divide the craft into classes according to the various lengths, say 30 in., 36 in., etc. This simple method has several drawbacks as it will be found that under the stress of competition the models, while remaining of the same length, will have increased in breadth, draught displacement and sail area. Where such a method is used it is necessary to add what are known as restrictions, that is to say that the various hull dimensions are restricted to certain sizes.

This method of measurement is at present in use by the Model Yachting Association for its 30 in. and 36 in. restricted classes.

36 IN. AND 30 IN. L.O.A. RESTRICTED CLASSES.

The dimensions of each class shall not exceed:—

	36 in. Class.		30 in. Class.
Length over all ..	.. 36 in.	..	.. 30 in.
Beam	.. 9 in.	..	.. 8 in.
Depth	.. 11 in.	..	.. 9 in.
Weight (not over)	.. 12 pounds	..	9 pounds

The length overall does not include rudder or bowsprit (if fitted). The depth is the distance between the highest point of the deck line (excluding fittings and bowsprit) and a line passing through the point of maximum draught parallel to the Load Water Line. Weight taken shall include largest suit of sails, spars, spinnaker and rudder.

Centreboards are prohibited.

Punts and Praams (i.e., all boats having forward transoms)

are prohibited.

There are also one or two other restrictions as to registration numbers on sails, etc. Full particulars can be found in the Sailing Rules of the Association.

These little craft have proved to be very capable little raters and they have the added advantages of portability and small cost. At the Championship Regatta of this class, held in 1936, there were 21 competitors representing seven different Clubs. The 36 in. Class is the more popular of the two and for anyone who is intending to take up model yacht racing in earnest is just the thing for a start.

THE MARBLEHEAD 50 IN.—800 CLASS.—This is a somewhat similar class of American origin but very popular over there and has been adopted by several Clubs in this country, but is not at present recognized by the Association.

The particulars of this Class are as follows:—

HULL RESTRICTIONS.—Hull 50 in. overall, 1/4 in. leeway either side of 50 in. measurement allowed. Movable keels, fin keels, centreboards, bilgeboards, lee boards, bowsprits and overhanging rudders are prohibited. Bumpers are not included in overall length but are limited to 1/2 in. overhang.

SAIL AREA MEASUREMENTS.—Sail area not to exceed 800 square inches. No fore triangle measurements, only actual sail measurements measured.

There are also restrictions on the diameter of spars and on the length and number of battens permitted on the sails. It is interesting to compare these two classes, the English and the American, and to note how the same result has been obtained by difference in measurements. In the English class, the sail spread is unrestricted, but the ability to carry sail is restricted by the weight being limited to 12 pounds and the depth to 11 in. The American craft can only carry 800 sq. in. of sail and the displacement is limited by the driving power of that sail. So far as is known the displacement of the average Marblehead Class Model is about 20 lb., but it will possibly be found that in future models this displacement will be exceeded.

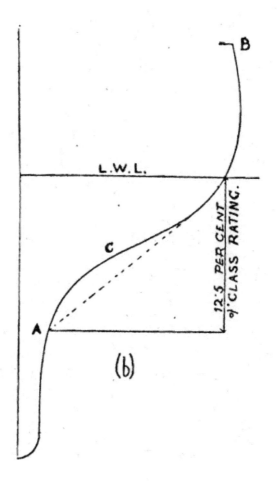

Fig. 10.

Model yachtsmen have generally followed the lead given by the prototype in the matter of rating rules, and one of the earliest rules used for rating yachts was that known as the 1730 Rule which is as follows:—

$$\frac{(\text{Length} + \text{Breadth})^2 \times \text{Breadth}}{1730} = \text{Tonnage}$$

It will be noticed in this rule how the breadth of beam is heavily taxed, the ultimate result being that yachts designed to rate under the rule increased in length, sail area and displacement but decreased in beam,what is known as the "plank on edge" type coming into use. This rule has been in use by model yachtsmen until quite recently but has now gone out of use. Here are the dimensions of two models of this type taken from a yachting paper published in 1907. Here is one with a L.W.L. of 47 in., a beam of 6 in., a draught of 11 in. with a displacement of 40 lb. and a sail area of 2,420 sq. in., while a later example is given having a L.W.L. of 57.25 in., a beam of 4.3 in., a draught of 16 in. and 2,410 sq. in. of sail with a displacement of 28 lb. It should be noted, however, that the first example is a keel boat but that the second one is of the fin and bulb keel type.

The 1730 Rule was abandoned by the Yacht Racing Association in 1887 in favour of what was known as the Length and Sail Area rule, $\frac{\text{Length} \times \text{Sail Area,}}{6,000}$ where length is the length on the Load Water Line when the load is fully loaded and in racing trim and the Sail Area is the total area of the sail spread measured according to certain prescribed directions. This rule is easy to understand and measure and is still the most popular amongst model yachtsmen. The Model Yachting Association in 1935 decided to follow the method of sail measurement used by full-size craft, and instead of taking the full area of the fore triangle as hitherto, only 85 per cent. of this area was to be used when calculating the rating. This had the effect of giving approximately 100 sq. in. of increased sail and it was found that boats which had previously been able to carry their rated sail area could not do so when given the increased sail spread, particularly as it was given the form of what is known as the Bermudian, which is comparatively high and narrow. The result was that the older type of 10-rater (the most generally used class) had to be given an increased displacement in order to carry a heavier weight of ballast, so that the modern 10-rater will be found to have a L.W.L. of from 48 in. to 50 in. and a sail area of 1,200 to 1, 240 in., while the displacement has been increased to anything up to 28 lb. The 10-rater designs given in this book will therefore require to have an increased displacement if they are to be used at the present time. Take, for instance, the design of *XPDNC* which has a displacement of 15 lb. and consider if the displacement can be increased in any way without affecting the general balance of the hull. The way to do so is to increase the spacing of the cross sections making them, say, 3.5 in. apart for a 42 in. L.W.L. and a displacement of approximately 20 lb.; or even by increasing the spacing to 4 in. with the resulting L.W.L. of 48 in. and an overall length of 80 in. as shown in Fig. 10, where it will be seen that the keel profile is altered and the sail area as shown in the sail plan has been reduced to 1,245 sq. in. See also the chapter on "built-up" models where the elongated design has been used for building directions. The design of the Schooner *Prospero* can also be used for a 10-rater.

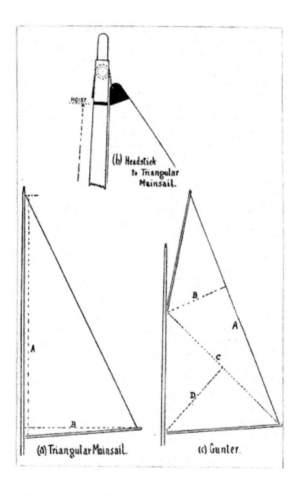

Fig. 11.—M.Y.A. sail area measurement

Defects of Length and Sail Area Rule

The Length and Sail Area rule was found to have several defects when applied to full-size yachts. One of these was that it only measured the L.W.L. length while the yacht was upright. It was found that by carrying out the ends of the yacht above water in what are known as overhangs that the rule could be evaded and the sailing length greatly increased when the yacht was heeled by the pressure of the wind on her sails. This principle of getting untaxed length was carried out to the greatest extent in what was known as the "Scow" type. Here the design of the hull was such that when heeled to any extent the boat practically sailed on one edge. The hull was made of a broad flat shallow shape with long flat overhanging ends and when heeled over when under sail the sailing length was greatly increased.

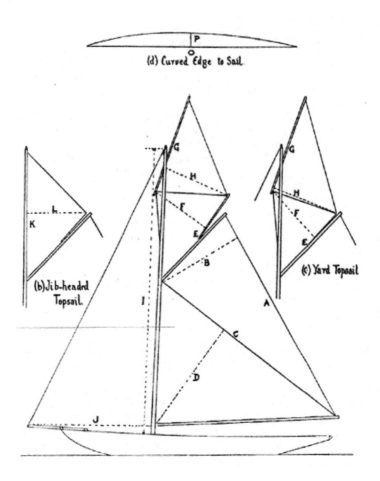

Fig. 12.—Sail area measurement of all M.Y.A. classes

Then, too, it was discovered that in the smaller classes it was not really necessary to carry any weight of ballast other than the crew who could by sitting up on the weather side utilize their weight to counterbalance the list caused by the pressure of the wind on the sails. Sufficient lateral resistance to enable the craft to go to windward could be secured by fitting a deep and narrow centreplate and the skimming dish sailing machine came into existence.

This is the type of craft those misinformed folk who decry the use of the Length and Sail Area rule for model yachts have in mind when they talk glibly of "sailing machines." It must not be forgotten when considering the suitability of any rating rule for model measuring purposes that the model cannot for obvious reasons be carried to such excess as the big craft.

The Yacht Racing Association later adopted what was known as the First Linear Rating Rule, 1896, where

$$\frac{L + B + \frac{3}{4}G + +\frac{1}{2}\sqrt{SA}}{2} = \text{Rating,}$$

and various alterations of this rule have been made, for instance in 1907 the rule was:

$$\frac{L + B + \frac{1}{2}C + 3d + \frac{1}{3}\sqrt{S.A.} - F.}{2} = \text{Rating,}$$

and about 1919 was replaced by:

$$\frac{L + \frac{1}{4}G + 2d + \sqrt{S.A.} - F.}{2.5} = \text{Rating.}$$

These rules introduced a new method of measurement in that the girth of the hull and the differences between the skin and chain girths were used, while in later instances the girth of the overhanging ends was added to the measured length, and in 1919 the length was measured not on the L.W.L. as had been done previously but at a height of 1.5 per cent. of the class rating above the L.W.L. At the same time various restrictions on the length of mast, draught and amount of tumble home of the topsides were added to the rule and these restrictions are still in force in the present International Rule adopted by the Model Yachting Association in 1934.

I.Y.R.U. FORMULA — OCTOBER, 1933

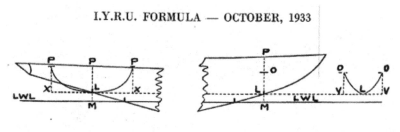

LM = 1·5 per cent. of Class Rating
PM = Freeboards at Bow and Stern as used for F measurement
OL = 5 per cent. of Class Rating
OLO — 2OV = Bow Girth Difference
PLP — 2PX = Stern Girth Difference

Figs. 13 and 14.—Method of measuring bow and stern girth differences

International Yacht Racing Union Formula

$$\frac{L + 2d + \sqrt{S.} - F.}{2.37} = \text{Rating.}$$

The length L of the formula is to be the length measured at a height of 1.5 per cent. of the class rating above the L.W.L. plus one and a half times the difference between the girth at the bow section measured to points 5 per cent. of the rating above "L" and twice the vertical height from "L" to those points plus one-third of the difference between the girth covering board to covering board at the stern ending of this length, and twice the vertical height at the side of the yacht at this station. The minimum difference of girth at the bow station as above defined to be 30 per cent. of twice the said vertical height.

Fig. 15.—"Gleam," "A" class

Note.—In the new rule 5 per cent. of rating above "L" shall be interpreted as 1.62 in. for 6-metre, and 1.9 in. for 12-metre models.

Fuller details giving the various restrictions for the two classes of I.Y.R.U. models recognized by the M.Y.A. will be found in the rule book for this class and all other classes published by the Association.

CHAPTER III

BUILDING A 36 in. MODEL YACHT BY THE CARVED HULL METHOD

THERE are two main methods of model hull carving and it may help the beginner if we briefly consider their respective virtues.

The Solid Block Method

This is the most elementary, and consists simply of carving the desired hull shape from a block of wood, and then hollowing it by "digging out" the inside. Whilst this has the advantage of simplicity it is really a laborious method and unless templates are constantly used to check the hull shape it is unlikely that both sides will be alike, a fault fatal to good sailing. It will be seen therefore, that apart from the fact that this method *sounds* simple it has really little to recommend it.

The "Bread and Butter" System

This is no more difficult than the solid block method, but produces a far more accurate type of hull. Furthermore, it uses less wood, is not so laborious, and is much more interesting. This is the ideal system for a beginner to adopt and many model yachtsmen remain faithful to it exclusively. It is the method selected for the building of the very attractive 36 in. model *Dawn* which is described in this chapter.

If a number of layers are cut out from smooth boards and fastened on top of each other we shall have a solid block of wood with steps on its sides and ends, as shown on page 42. Assuming that the layers were cut to their correct shapes before assembling, it will be seen that we have now only to cut away the steps to bring the hull to its true shape. This is much more interesting than hacking out a hull from a solid block, and, furthermore, we shall know that our hull is accurately shaped.

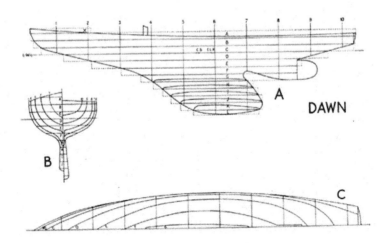

Fig. 16.—The lines of the 36-in. model yacht "Dawn" as described in this chapter.

We have now to consider how to get the shapes to which our various layers have to be cut and we must refer to the plans. If the reader will look at the design given in Fig. 16 he will see that there are three plans shown, lettered A. B, and C.

A is the side view or *profile plan.*

B is the end view or *body plan.*

C is the top view or *water-line plan.*

On the profile and body plans (*A* and B) it will be noticed that there are a number of parallel lines running horizontally across the drawings. These lines are called "water-lines" and represent the layers from which the boat will be built. Imagine for a moment that we took a sharp knife and cut our hull along these lines. We should get a number of layers which would progressively get smaller as we worked towards the keel. The shapes of these layers are shown in the water-line plan and are lettered A,B,C, etc., consecutively. The actual line on which the yacht floats is known as the load water-line and is marked L.W.L. on drawing A.

In the water-line plan, C, it will be seen that only one half of each layer shape is shown. This is accepted practice in Naval Architecture and is simply to obviate unnecessary work, as obviously both sides of the hull are alike. This principle of showing only one half of the hull is similarly followed in the body plan.

If we refer again to the profile plan we shall see that it is divided up into sections by 10 vertical lines and these section lines are numbered from bow to stern. If we were to cut through the hull at section 1, the shape we should get is shown on the body plan and marked 1. Similarly each shape shown on the body plan represents the shape of the hull at the section line of corresponding number.

It is generally worth while to make a full-sized drawing

of the profile and body plans before commencing to build a model as this ensures accuracy and avoids the annoying mistakes which frequently occur if measurements are taken from a small plan and multiplied up several times.

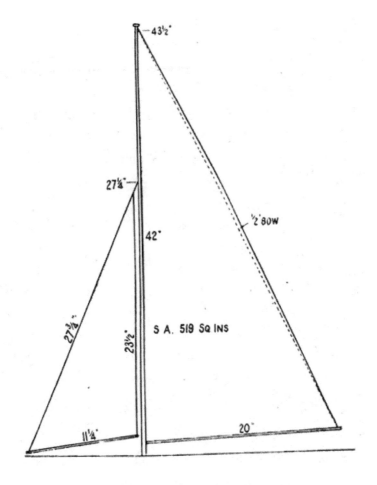

Fig. 17.—Sail plan of "Dawn."

This model is of a handy size. having a displacement of 7 lb. As the keel will weigh 4 1/4 lb. and the spars and sails about 1 lb., it will be seen that the weight of the hull should not exceed 1 3/4 lb.

The Timber Required

Apart from the plans the first consideration is the purchasing of timber. The best wood to use for all carved models is yellow (or white) pine, but this is not always easy to get. Cedar is also very good and sugar pine is also quite suitable. Ordinary red pine can be used if well-seasoned and free from knots, but yellow pine and cedar are easier to work and lighter in weight.

In the design of *Dawn* the water-lines are three-quarters of an inch apart and so our wood must be exactly three-quarters of an inch thick when "finished" (i.e. planed and glass-papered ready for use). It will therefore be necessary to purchase timber one inch thick and have it planed down to three-quarters of an inch. The timber yard where the wood is purchased will "finish" it to any desired size and the slight extra cost of this is well worth while.

Before purchasing timber the amount required should be carefully calculated to avoid wastage, as frequently the surplus wood cut out of the top layers will provide material for the smaller ones. A table of the wood required to build *Dawn* is given to simplify matters for the novice.

Table of Timber Required

Layers A and B, each 36 in. long
Layer C, 35 in. long.   8 in. wide by 3/4 in. thick.
Layer D 30 in. long.

Layer E 24 in. long.

Layer X 8 in. long, 6 in. wide, 1/2 in. thick.

Layers F. G, H, I, J, K, can all be obtained from the waste wood cut out from the centre of the other layers.

Deck 37 in. long, 8 in. wide, 1/8 in. thick, pine.

Mast 48 in. by 1/2 in. square, pine. Main boom, 23 in. by 3/8 in square.

Fore Boom, 13 in., by 1/4 in. square.

Marking Out the Layers

On obtaining the wood the first stage is to mark out on the layers the shapes of the various water-lines. First draw a centre line on each layer and with the aid of a carpenter's square carry the line across the ends of the layers and join up down the other side so that the centre line runs right around each board.

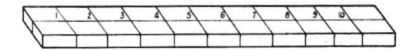

Fig. 18.—A board marked with section lines.

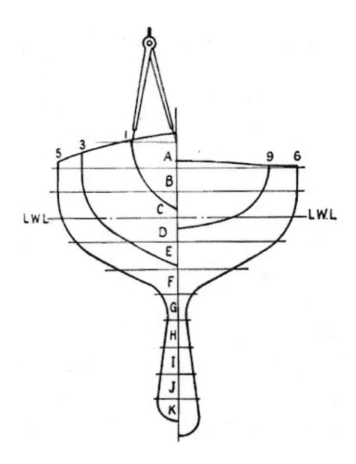

Fig. 19.—The use of dividers to transfer widths from body plan to layers.

Then take layer A and mark the section lines across it. It will be seen from the plan that this layer starts approximately three inches forward of section 1. We shall therefore draw a section line 1 on our board three in. from its forward end.

Draw this section line across the board taking care to get it at right-angles to the centre line. Section line 2 is then put in 3 1/2 in. from Section 1 and the remaining section lines are similarly drawn. Each of these lines is then extended around the board so that the board then has the centre line and the section lines on both its faces. The layer should now be clearly marked with its identifying letter, and Fig. 18 illusstrates a layer thus prepared.

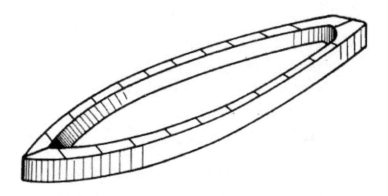

Fig. 20.—A layer shaped ready for assembly.

We are now ready to draw in the water-lines preparatory to cutting out the various layers and it should be understood that whenever reference is made to the shape of a layer, it is the upper face that is being referred to. Start with layer A and have before you the full-size body plan of the model. Take a pair of dividers and place point at the one point at the intersection of the centre line and water-line A. The other point of the dividers is now brought to where Section 1 cuts the water-line A, as shown in Fig. 19; this is the half width of the hull at Section 1. Transfer the dividers to Section 1 on the plank and prick off this distance on both sides of the centre line. Next, prick off the distance from the centre line to Section 2 on the body plan and transfer this to the plank. So continue with each of the sections, being careful to work on water-line A all the while, and not to stray on to one of the other water-lines in error.

We now have to put in the point on the centre-line where the bow meets it. We therefore refer to our profile plan and measure the distance from Section 1 to the bow. This distance is then transferred to our board, and the stern is then treated similarly, this time measuring backwards from Section 10.

It will be seen that if a curve is now drawn through all the marks pricked on our layer, the shape of the required water-line will be produced. To draw the curve through the prick marks, use a "batten." This is a straight flexible piece of wood and is bent to touch all the marks and a line is drawn in by pencil. A suitable batten would be about 3 ft. 6 in. long by 1/2 in. by 1/8 in. Each layer is treated like this in turn. In order to get the extra height needed at the bow it is necessary to use a short extra layer and this is marked X in Fig. 16A.

It should be noted that the complete fin and keel are built up and carved in wood and that at a later stage the keel is cut off and forms the pattern from which the lead keel is cast. Whilst the keel can then be secured with screws, it is much more satisfactory to use motor cycle spokes which pass right up through the fin and are screwed up tight on the inside of the hull by the spoke nipples. In order to obviate the difficulty of boring long fine holes truly vertical, the positions of the spokes should be marked out on each layer so that each layer may be drilled separately before assembly. If the position of the spoke holes is marked on both sides of each layer, the holes can be drilled through from one side, after which the layer is turned over and the holes drilled through from the other side. This will ensure the holes being truly vertical and the holes should be drilled before proceeding further. A 1/8 in. diameter drill produces the correct sized hole for the 10 gauge spokes which we shall use.

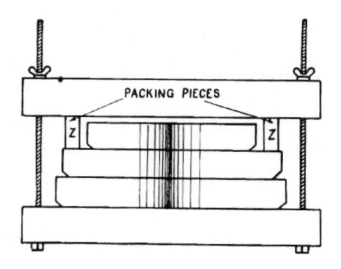

Fig. 21.—Layers in cramp during "glueing-up" process.

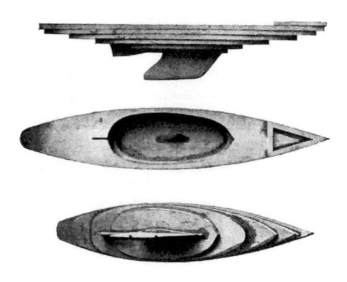

A carved-out model, during construction

Cutting the Layers to Shape

The various layers may now be cut to shape using a bow saw or a pad saw. In sawing out the layers, keep 1/8 in. outside the water-line. Then take a plane or chisel and chamfer off the top edge of the layer exactly to the water-line. If the layers were all cut to exact size and assembled, the slightest mistake made in the drawing-in of the curves would probably spoil the hull. By following the method advocated, however, one is left with a little wood to "play with," and the surplus is cleaned off when carving the hull to shape. In cutting out the layers, the section lines marked on the edges of the layers will have been removed and these should now be put in again.

It will be seen that if the layers were now assembled, a solid block hull would be formed and a great deal of hard work with a gouge would be required to hollow it out. Much of the surplus wood, however, can be removed at this stage by sawing out the centres of the layers, as shown in Fig. 20, Then, after assembling, it will simply be a matter of removing the "steps," as on the outside of the hull.

To ascertain the amount of wood which can be removed, take layer A and place it on layer B face downwards, bringing the centre-lines and section lines into correct alignment, and then, with a sharp pencil, run around the outline of layer B. tilting the pencil to get under the chamfer. This gives the shape of the underside of layer A, which, of course, is the same as the top side of layer B. We must therefore deduct the thickness which the finished hull is to be before doing any cutting out. It will be found satisfactory if 1/4 in. thickness is allowed at the sides and 1 1/4 in. at bow and stern. These distances are therefore marked in inside the line already drawn and a fresh line put in.

Theoretically, the centre of the layer may now be cut out to this line, but in practice it is wise to leave more wood to take the stress of cramping up during the glueing together of the layers. Therefore, cut well inside this line, leaving not less than 1 in. of wood at any point. Use the bow saw or pad saw, first drilling a hole in the waste part of the wood to admit the saw blade. After removing the waste wood, chamfer the inner edge of the layer back to the mark line, and this will be a very useful guide when hollowing out the hull, as it shows when the desired hull thickness is reached.

Glueing Up the Layers

Having prepared all the layers, we are now ready to consider glueing up. Originally, good quality Scotch glue was used and after the hull was glued up all joints were "sewn" with copper wire. This was a very tedious job and since the introduction of Casein glue it has fortunately become quite unnecessary. This glue is enormously strong and is waterproof. It is in the form of a powder and is mixed with cold water preparatory to use. Most handicraft shops and ironmongers sell this glue, principally under the trade name of "Casco." Joints made with this glue will never give trouble, as if properly made and protected by paint, they are actually stronger than the wood itself.

It is essential that the layers are glued up under pressure and some form of cramps are therefore necessary. As only one layer is added at a time, it is possible to dispense with cramps by using ordinary wood screws put into parts of the wood which will later be hollowed out, but this method is far inferior to the use of cramps as shown in Fig. 21. These are very easily made as they merely consist of pieces of wood 1 in. square and pieces of screwed rod with nuts. As previously mentioned, only one layer must be added at a time as, otherwise, distortion and probable breakage of the hull will result. As the lowest layer is smaller than those above it, any pressure put upon it would tend to force it down through the other layers, the sides of which would be forced outwards.

Having mixed the Casein glue in accordance with the directions on the tin, take the layers E and F and put a thin even layer of glue on each. Then put together, taking care to get the centre-line and the section lines of the two pieces to coincide. Now apply the cramps, evenly spaced along the work, putting one near each end. Tighten up evenly and gradually, carefully checking the alignment of the layers. This is most important as any lack of alignment will upset the whole shape of the hull, so take care, and if necessary slacken off the pressure and begin again. Allow to stand for 12 to 24 hours before removing the cramps.

Layer D may now be added in exactly the same way, but packing pieces shown "Z" in Fig. 21 must be used when cramping up to put the pressure on the joint being made. It will be noticed that the cramp does not then touch the small layer at all. After each layer dries, a further one may be added to the block until it is completed.

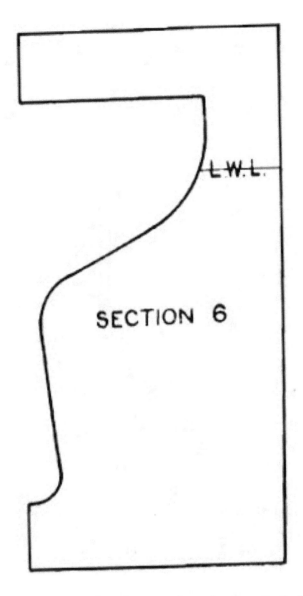

Fig. 22.—Template for use when shaping the hull

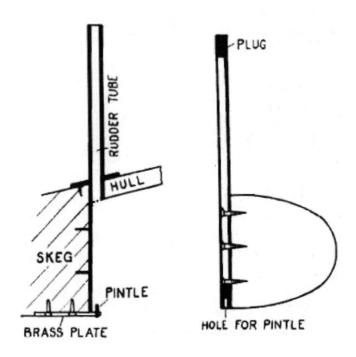

Fig. 23.—Details of rudder tube and rudder, showing method of fixing

It may here be stated that you cannot get a perfect joint from the surface that is left by the planing machine. Each layer should therefore be left a little full and then surfaced up with a plane set very fine before marking out the water-lines.

Shaping the Hull

The great secret of shaping a boat after the glueing up stage is finished is gradually to carve away the superfluous wood, keeping the whole about as much the same stage of finish as possible. Chisel, plane and spokeshave may be used until the boat is within about 1/16 in. of the finished shape. The fairing can now be done by means of coarse glass-paper wrapped around a thin piece of flexible wood or tin. The rubbing, as also the use of cutting tools, should always be done in the direction of the diagonals. The finishing should be done with fine glass-paper, at which stage the joints, if good, should disappear, or at least be only hair-lines on the surface. Full size half-breadth templates should be made and offered to the hull while shaping. These templates are cardboard or thin wood patterns of the various section shapes, one being shown in Fig. 22. It will suffice if a template is made for each alternate section. Mark the L.W.L. on the templates and this should register the L.W.L. joint line on the hull when the template is applied.

After shaping the outside, the section marks, which are still visible on the top of layer A, should be squared off on to the ship's sides and used for marking out the points of sheer. It should be explained that the "sheer" is the curved deckline running from bow to stern. On the profile plan it is easy to measure the distance from the sheer line to the top of the layer and this should be done on each section line. It should be remembered, however, to reduce the hull side by another 1/8 in,, which is the thickness of the deck. When these points have been put in, a line is drawn through them with the aid of the batten, and the surplus wood is then carved away with chisel and spokeshave. To "finish" the top of the hull use glass-paper wrapped around a round stick which can rest across both gunwales.

The superfluous wood inside the hull is now removed. For this purpose a spoon gouge is necessary and a small plane with a curved sole is very useful if available. Proceed until the grooves formed by the chamfered edges of the board disappear, and the inside of the hull can then be finished with glass-paper wrapped around a cork.

The Rudder

Having finished the hull, the rudder tube can now be fitted. The distance from the rudder pintle to the top of the deck is 4 1/2 in. and about 1/8 in. should be left above deck. The tube is therefore 4 5/8 in. long, and is about 1/4 in. outside diameter, and of brass. The height of the skeg being 2 3/4 in., the remainder of the tube should be cut away until only a strip 2-10 in. wide is left. This should be drilled with fine holes at about 1 in. intervals and the holes countersunk.

Drill the hull to receive the tube and the back of the skeg should be slightly hollowed with rat-tail file to allow the strip to seat properly. Fine brass screws are used to fix it in position, white lead being used between wood and metal. Cut a thin brass plate about 7/8 in. diameter with an oval hole so that it passes over the rudder tube and lies flat on the wood of the hull (inside). This is now soldered to the tube and two small brass screws secure the washer in position in the hull. Now take a piece of brass rod or tube 5 1/4 in. long, which is a good easy fit in the rudder tube, and this will form the rudder stem. The rudder blade is cut from 1/4 in. mahogany and tapered off towards its rear edge. Its front edge is now hollowed to fit the rudder stem which is secured to it with fine screws. A small hole is drilled in the bottom end of the rudder stem so that it may fit down on the pintle. The pintle is a small piece of brass wire soldered into a brass plate which is then screwed to the bottom of the skeg. Fig. 23 should make all rudder details clear.

Fitting the Keel

The lead keel should now be cast and fitted. First draw the lead line on the fin. as shown in Fig. 24. Provided the fin has been carved accurately this should give a keel of correct weight. Should it later be found that the model is not on an even keel when floated, a small block of lead may be secured inside the hull, near bow or stern as necessary, to produce the correct trim.

Cut off the keel pattern on this line using a fine-toothed saw. From this pattern a simple plaster mould may be made and the keel cast. If this is beyond the reader's capabilities, he can easily get the keel cast at a foundry. Short ends cut off the spokes may be used as cores for leaving the holes in the lead when casting, but if this has not been done, the holes may be drilled with an ordinary twist drill if plenty of turpentine is used to lubricate the drill. The joint between lead and fin should be well luted with paint when keel is being fitted.

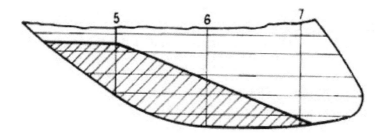

Fig. 24.—Diagram of lead keel of "Dawn"

Deck beams are now fitted to support the deck and give it camber. They are cut from pine 3/8 in. thick and are shaped as shown in Fig. 25, from which it will be seen that the top face is slightly curved. They should be about 3/8 in. deep, plus the camber, and are secured with brass screws as shown.

It is most desirable to fit an adjustable mast slide as the exact mast position can only be determined by experiment. Details of a mast slide are given in a subsequent chapter. The mast step should be screwed in position on the floor of the hull before proceeding further.

The deck may be cut out of 1/8 in. pine. If it is bent and held into position on the deck beams, a pencil can be run around the outside of the hull and will mark out the deck shape. Cut about 1/4 in. outside this line, and do not clean up to shape until after the deck is fitted. Pieces of 1/8 in. mahogany should be cut out and glued and screwed to the underside of the deck to reinforce it at the mast position.

The inside of the hull, the deck beams, and the underside of the deck should now be given three coats of varnish. The deck may next be lined-out with a sharp pencil and batten, to represent planking, and a spacing of about 1/4 in. looks very well. Then apply a coat of varnish immediately to prevent the deck becoming soiled.

The deck is fitted after holes have been drilled for the rudder tube and mast tube; the latter hole is of course a slot. Brass screws or veneer pins are used to secure the deck, the joint being well luted with white lead and gold size to make it waterproof. The deck may now be cleaned down until exactly flush with the hull sides.

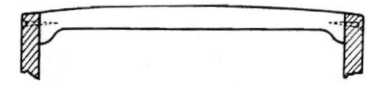

Fig. 25.—Deck beam fitted

Painting and Finishing

Rub down the outside of the hull with fine glass-paper and two thin coats of priming paint may then be given, rubbing down with flour glass-paper between each. After each coat of paint, the L.W.L. joint should be kept in view by going over it with a copying-ink pencil. Strips of gummed paper about 1/4 in. wide should be cut and stuck around the L.W.L. while the topsides and under-body are having the colours put on, and when soaked off should leave a dead sharp line. "Robbialac" Synthetic Finish will be found excellent and is quick-drying, or flat colours and varnish may be used if preferred.

Finally, a beading of mahogany 1/4 in. wide, 1/8 in. thick, is bent to follow the deck-line and is secured near the deck edge with fine brass pins. This represents the covering board of a full size yacht and greatly adds to the model's appearance. The deck is then given two more coats of varnish, and the model is ready for "fitting out."

CHAPTER IV

BUILDING A MODEL 10-RATER

IN this Chapter the building of a successful 10-rater model known as *XPDNC* is described. The reader who desires to build this model is advised carefully to study the methods of construction explained for the model *Dawn* in Chapter III. The "bread-and-butter" system of hull construction is used for each boat, and the methods described for *Dawn* may be equally well applied to the present model. This chapter also contains the lines and sail-plan for the 10-rater *Electra*, a type of boat specially designed for sailing on waters where weeds prevail.

In order for the scheme of this boat, *XPDNC* to be carried out, she must have 9 lb. of lead in her keel. As she is only 15 lb. displacement, it is necessary to reduce the weight of hull, sails and fittings complete to 6 lb. In order to do this the shell of the hull must be reduced to at least 2 1/2 lb., including fin.

Table of "Offsets"

Before proceeding further, it may perhaps be advisable to explain the use of the Table of "Offsets,". In the sheer plan of the design all measurements are taken from the L.W.L., up or down, as the case may be. For instance, the sections are in the first vertical column, and along the top are the various lines of the boats.

If the profile depth at section No. 9 is required, place your finger under the section in first column, and run it along until under the column headed "profile," and the depth required is found. The deck height or depth of any buttock can be found in the same way.

TABLE OF OFFSETS FOR MODEL YACHT *XPDNC*

	HEIGHTS AND DEPTHS FROM L.W.L.							HALF BREADTHS.												
Sections	Deck	Pro-file	B1	B2	B3	B4	B5	Deck	A	B	C	D	E	F	L.W.L. G	H	I	J	K	L
Bow	4.0	4.0	..	..	..	..		..	0.9	0.9	0.5									
1	3.82	1.62	3.82	..	..	..		1.0	0.9	0.9	0.5									
2	3.67	1.0	1.3	..	..	..		1.9	1.85	1.65	..									
3	3.5	0.5	0.6	1.0	..	..		2.75	2.7	2.6	2.0									
4	3.37	..	0.75	0.27	0.9	..		3.5	3.5	3.4	3.1									
5	3.25	0.5	0.42	0.3	0.02	1.5		4.15	4.15	4.05	3.9	2.9								
6	3.1	1.0	0.92	0.8	0.55	..		4.7	4.7	4.65	4.5	4.0								
7	3.0	2.5	1.36	1.23	1.04	0.67	0.9	5.18	5.18	5.15	5.0	4.7	3.15	0.05						
8	2.9	5.7	1.7	1.6	1.42	1.1	0.27	5.5	..	5.4	5.4	5.15	4.2	0.35	0.2	0.1	0.1			
9	2.8	8.0	1.92	1.8	1.65	1.35	0.78	5.8	..	5.8	5.7	5.5	4.7	0.8	0.3	0.25	0.27	0.35	0.4	
10	2.7	8.5	2.0	1.9	1.75	1.5	1.0	5.95	..	5.95	5.85	5.7	5.0	1.0	0.3	0.27	0.32	0.45	0.6	0.6
11	2.65	8.8	1.95	1.85	1.75	1.5	1.02	6.0	..	6.0	5.9	5.75	5.1	0.8	0.2	0.15	0.2	0.3	0.5	0.5
12	2.6	8.95	1.73	1.7	1.58	1.45	0.9	5.97	..	5.97	5.87	5.7	4.9	0.35	..		0.1	0.25	0.3	
13	2.55	8.5	1.4	1.37	1.25	1.1	0.65	5.8	..	5.8	5.75	5.5	4.25	0.15	..					
14	2.5	3.85	0.97	0.95	0.85	0.7	0.2	5.6	..	5.6	5.5	5.2	0.25	0.1	..					
15	2.5	4.0	0.5	0.47	0.4	0.2	0.5	5.27	..	5.27	5.15	4.45	..	0.1	..					
16	2.5	..	..	0.02	0.13	0.35	..	4.85	..	4.85	4.7									
17	2.5	0.5	0.5	0.52	0.65	0.65	1.0	4.3	..	4.3	4.0									
18	2.55	1.0	1.0	1.05	1.2	..	..	3.7	..	3.7										
19	2.6	1.5	1.5	1.6	2.6	..	..	3.0	..	2.95										
Tran-som	2.7	2.7	..	2.0	..	..	..	2.3	..											

Buttocks spaced 1 in. from amidship line. Length over all 60 in.
Water Line spaced 1 in. from Load Water Line. Length L.W.L. 36 in.
Overhangs 12 in. each.

In the half-breadth plan the distances are measured from the centre line of boat, and appear in the columns headed "half-breadths" In the body plan both the depths, heights, and half-breadths appear.

It will be seen, therefore, that a boat could be transferred to paper merely from the Table of "Offsets."

From your table of offsets make a full-sized drawing of the profile and also of the body plan.

Marking Out the Lines

The layer (A) will be 59 1/2 in. long. 12 in. wide, and 1 in. thick; upon this layer mark a central line on either side right down the plank. This layer A starts 1/2 in. behind the foremost point of the hull. Therefore, as our sections are spaced 3 in. apart, the first section will be 2 1/2 in. from the end of board. Draw lines representing the section square to the central line, and from the table of offsets lay off the various half-breadths, afterwards sweeping a line through these points by means of a lancewood or red pine batten, held down by means of weights. You will notice that all the measurements are given in inches and tenths of inches, and a suitable scale rule should be obtained. You will also be able to obtain the layer E from the centre of this plank; the same cross section lines being used. B layer will be 58 in. long, C 48 in. long and D, which is the load water line, will, of course, be exactly 36 in. Layer F will be carried right back into the after fin, the rest of which will be made up from a piece of 2-10ths in. thick.

Cutting Out the Layers

Choose a section near amidships, section 10 for preference, and square off vertical lines on edge of each board, joining them up across the other face of each layer. Now cut just outside the water-lines, or, better still, take them to a steam fret sawyer, not band sawyer. Ask the sawyer to see that the saw is cutting dead vertical with table. The fin should be made up from layers in a similar manner, the lower portion indicated by the top of lead line being afterwards cut off and replaced by the keel of which this will provide the pattern. Each piece in the fin should be drilled separately for the spokes to pass through, the spots being measured off and squared on sides of layers to ensure accuracy. The best plan in drilling layers of fin is to start on top, drilling about half-way and meeting the hole from the under face. An extra piece (M) 20 in. long will be required to bring up the sheer line to its required height. Before glueing up the layers, and in order to have guidance as to thickness when carving out the inside, lines should be drawn on the under face of each layer representing the shape of the joint shown on the inside of boat when finished. For instance, the profile line of *XPDNC* rises at an angle with the water of one in six; therefore, if the hull was to be 1 in thick when carved out this joint would be 6 in. broad at the profile. As the hull is only to be 2-10ths in. when finished, the breadth of the joint on the profile will be 1.2 in. broad, gradually narrowing down until it reaches the mid section, where, if the sides are more or less vertical, it will be the same breadth as the finished thickness of hull. In order to detect this line before you have cut too far when carving out, a small groove is cut round the inside of this line. The idea of this is not so much to give the finished thickness, but to give a guide as to how far you are from the outside. After having cut down to the inside grooves, you can then go all over the hull with a concave plane, until you have reduced the shell to the required weight.

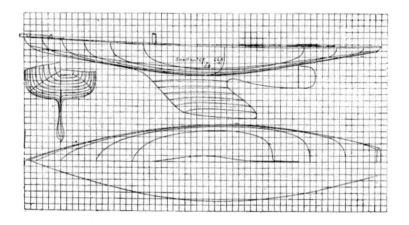

Fig. 26.—Lines of "XPDNC" (1 inch squares)

Before shaping the outside the after fin piece should be glued on and also the fin and lead. You can then use the flat of the layers to place the square upon, to see that all is square to the load water line, which is, of course, very important.

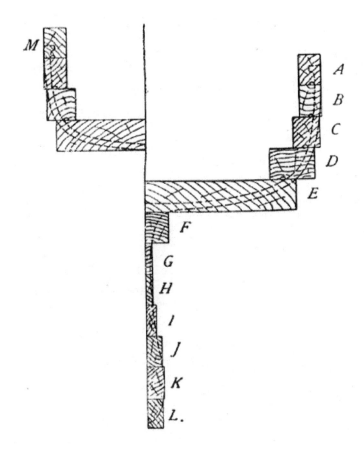

**Fig. 27.—Cross sections of "bread-and-butter"
construction, showing the guiding groove for interior
carving**

In making up the fin all the pieces should be got up square
and the sections marked on face and sides; then drill each piece
separately for the spokes, and lay off the profile on the face.

You will have to cut out these layers to the water-lines with a chisel, as sawing would cut away too much of the under face which is, in the case of the lower layers, wider than the top face. The spokes in the case of *XPDNC* will be 12 gauge, 7 1/2 and 8 1/2 in. in length; about 1 1/2 in. of thread is required, as they will have to be cut down again after lower plank has been cut out on the inside.

Layers are referred to as A, B, C, etc., starting from top full-length layer

Fig. 28.—Showing construction of "bread-and-butter" hull

Glueing the Layers

It is absolutely essential that all your layers should be glued together exactly in the positions relative to each other, (see instructions in Chapter III). First take the layers D and E, which together will form the under-water body of the boat. Lines square to the section have already been marked on the edge to guide for the fore and aft position, and also lines joining the two midship lines on each face of the layers should be drawn on the edge at either end.

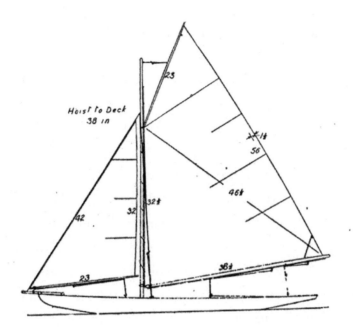

Fig. 29.—Sail plan—"XPDNC"

The layers A and B may also be glued together. Use Casein glue. Then glue the layer C on to B, and layer F on to layer E. The layers D, E, and F, should then be brought together with A, B and C. Finally, the piece we will call M must be glued on to make up the sheer. The reason for adopting this particular method of glueing up instead of starting with A and B, and going right on is to avoid breaking joints already made, as would be done through the wood having been cut out of the inside of the upper layers, there then being nothing to take the direct pressure which would be exerted in glueing the layer F, for instance. It may be here repeated that you cannot get a perfect joint from the surface that is left by the planing machine. Each layer should be left a little full and surfaced up with a trying plane set very fine before marking out the waterlines. The keel should now be cast and fitted. Firstly, cut off the pattern. If this were done exactly to the line indicated by the top of lead, you would lose something by the saw cut and the keel would not fit properly. In order to avoid this, a line about 1/4 in. lower should be marked and the pattern cut off at this point. Shoot the top face of pattern straight and square and glue on a piece of 3/8 in. thick and shape down to top face. The short ends cut off from spokes may be used as cores for leaving the holes in lead when casting. Your lead will now be a little full of the required weight, which is 9 lb. The part of the fin left on will also be full, and both should be shot to the designed line, and the keel fitted, white lead being used between the joint.

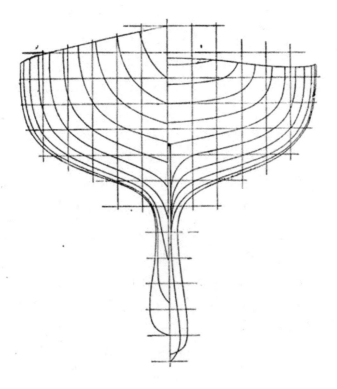

Fig. 30.—10-rater "Electra" (body plan)

The stern tube should next be fitted. The distance from rudder pintle to top of deck is 6 3/4 in.; about 1/8 should be left above deck. The tube should therefore be 6 7/8 in. over all. The length of stern-post being 3 3/8 in. the remainder of the tube should be cut away until only a strip 2-10ths in. wide, which is the width of the stern-post, is left; drill holes every inch in this strip, starting from lower end about 3/8 in. from the pintle and countersink them. Cut a thin brass plate about 1 1/4 in. diameter with an oval hole, so that it passes over the stern tube and lies flat on the wood of the hull (inside). The stern-post should be hollowed out with a rat-tail file to allow the strip to seat properly. Screw the stern-tube temporarily in position and solder plate on, seeing that the latter is flat in inside of the hull. The stern-tube may now be fitted permanently, white lead being used between wood and metal.

The deck beams, if spaced 9 in. apart from bow, will just miss the mast, hatch and stern-tube. The beams should be cut to the required curvature, the amount of rise being indicated in the drawing by the mid-deck line.

Using a fixed radius and depending upon the shorter breadth of deck beams to reduce the height of rise is not correct, as beams 3 and 4, for instance, are about the same breadth, but No. 3 is only about two-thirds the rise of No. 4. The beams, 1/4 in. X 1/4 in. mahogany, should be let in to a stringer 5-16ths in. X 3/8 in. running round the topsides, inside. Do not simply saw out a piece from the topsides and drop them in, as you will always have them showing, and this looks bad. Before putting the deck on the mast steps should be screwed in position.

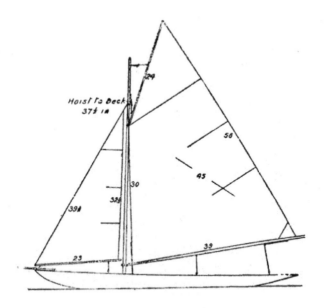

Fig. 31.—Sail plan of "Electra"

The deck should be of pine 3-32nds in. in thickness. Cut out pieces of 1/8 in. mahogany to reinforce underside of deck at hatch and mast slide. These should be glued on the underside before cutting out the apertures, and will prevent the deck splitting when the latter is being done.

Draw a line representing the amidships and drill small holes for 1/4 in. No. 0 screws at positions where deck beams occur.

TABLE OF OFFSETS FOR *ELECTRA*.

HEIGHTS AND DEPTHS.

Sections	Deck	Profile	B1	B2	B3	B4	B5
Bow	4.0	4.0					
1	3.8	2.0	3.45				
2	3.6	1.0	1.55	3.6			
3	3.4	0.2	0.57	1.25			
4	3.27	0.5	0.2	0.2	1.1	1.3	
5	3.12	1.25	0.9	0.52	0.7	0.6	0.75
6	3.0	2.25	1.53	1.53	1.15	0.97	0.2
7	2.9	3.5	2.02	1.85	1.45	1.2	0.5
8	2.8	5.1	2.32	2.02	1.63	1.35	0.7
9	2.7	6.75	2.52	2.1	1.72	1.3	0.75
10	2.6	8.0	2.6	2.1	1.75	1.05	0.65
11	2.5	8.72	2.4	1.95	1.4	0.7	0.45
12	2.45	9.0	2.07	1.3	1.4	0.2	
13	2.42	9.25	1.7	0.8	1.03	0.45	0.8
14	2.4	4.05	1.6	0.2	0.55	1.35	
15	2.42	4.5	1.05	0.45	0.02		
16	2.42	0.6	0.41	0.45	0.7		
17	2.45	0.25	0.3	1.15	1.5		
18	2.47	1.0	1.0	1.87			
19	2.6	1.75	1.77				
Transom	2.75	2.75	2.5				

HALF BREADTHS.

Sections	Deck	A	B	C	D	E	L.W.L. F	G	H	I	J	K	L
Bow	1.1												
1	2.0	0.8											
2	2.9	1.87											
3	3.55	2.8	1.4	1.7	1.55								
4	4.17	3.55	2.5	2.94	3.0	0.8							
5	4.73	4.2	3.4	3.75	4.0	2.3	0.2						
6	5.17	4.73	4.12	4.55	4.62	3.27	1.075	0.2					
7	5.54		4.7	5.075	5.1	4.0	1.65	0.5	0.25	0.1			
8	5.77		5.15	5.43	5.36	4.36	2.1	0.65	0.42	0.43	0.4	0.8	0.7
9	5.9		5.52	5.68	5.52	4.55	2.25	0.7	0.5	0.53	0.7	0.67	0.4
10	6.0		5.75	5.73	5.6	4.6	1.83	0.6	0.37	0.4	0.5	0.3	
11	5.95		5.9	5.9	5.85	4.45	1.12	0.4	0.1	0.1	0.2		
12	5.82		6.0	5.85	5.35	4.1	0.46	0.2					
13	5.53		5.95	5.7	5.0	3.1	0.17	0.13					
14	5.55		5.82	5.45	4.3	1.1	0.1	0.1					
15	5.2		5.53	5.07	2.9								
16	4.72		5.2	4.52									
17	4.22		4.74	3.6									
18	3.52		4.2										
19	2.85		3.45										
Transom	1.8		2.25										

L.O.A = 60 in.   Overhang 10 in. each end.

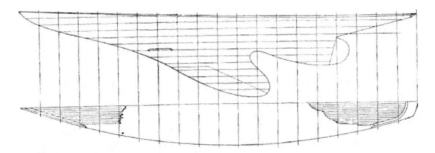

This boat was specially designed for ponds in which weeds prevail

Fig. 32.—Profile and deck-line of 10-rater "Electra"

Give the underside of deck two coats of french polish and two of varnish, and also the inside of hull. Cut out the deck roughly to shape, about within 1/4 in. all round. Cut out hatchway and mast slot.

In order to get the indian ink lines representing deck planking to stand and not run, it is necessary to give the wood three or four coats of patent size. This is best done before dealing with the underside as it will keep the top of deck clean and can be more easily glass-papered than when the reinforcements are on the underside.

The deck may now be fitted, screws or veneer pins being used to hold it down. White lead mixed with gold size should be used to seal it with the topsides.

For painting and finishing the hull follow the instructions given for *Dawn* in Chapter III.

CHAPTER V

THE CONSTRUCTION OF "BUILT-UP" OR
PLANKED YACHTS

"BUILT-UP" is a term used in contradistinction to "dugout" or "cut-out" and means that the model is built up with planking and frames, etc., in practically the same way as a full-sized yacht.

There are many ways of planking a boat, but those generally used for models may be sub-divided into two classes, viz., single or double planking.

Single planking is generally laid "carvel," the planks being laid longitudinally edge to edge, the watertightness of the hull depending, in the case of a small boat, on the excellence of the close laid joints.

With this method of planking the "frames" or "ribs" can be either "bent" or "cut." A "bent frame" explains itself, but a "cut frame" is one that is sawn to shape to fit the cross section of the model. The difference in the construction of these two methods is that the bent frames are usually added after the hull is planked up, the hull being built-up on "shadows" or "moulds," the ribs being bent to fit the inside shape of the hull. The ribs or "frames" between the shadows are fitted first and, finally, the shadows are removed one by one and replaced by ribs.

When cut or sawn frames are used, shadows or moulds are not necessary, the planks being laid on the frames which are erected on and secured to the keel or keelson.

It is of course, possible to combine the two methods and to use sawn frames with intermediate bent frames.

DOUBLE SKIN.—In this case the planking is laid in two thicknesses, as the name implies, one skin being laid vertically or diagonally, and the other, generally the outer skin, laid longitudinally. There are also variants of this method in which both skins are laid diagonally.

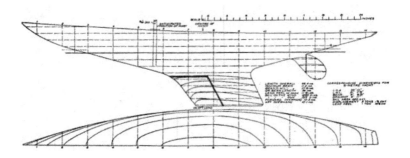

Fig. 33.—Design for a 1 2/3rd in. to the foot 6-meter yacht

Whatever the kind of skin it is necessary to have some kind of framework on which the hull is built. There is the keel or keelson, the stern and the stern-post, the deadwood, the counter timber and the stern transom.

Fig. 35 shows the construction plan of a 10-rating model. This drawing is that of the elongated *XPDNC*, referred to in the chapter on rating rules. It will be noted that the bent keel extends in one piece from the turn of the stern-post at section to the stern transom, the fin keel is added after the hull has been planked.

Making the Moulds

The first thing to do is to make the moulds or shadows on which the boat is to be planked. These are usually recommended to be cut out of one piece of wood of about 3/8 in. in thickness, but a better way is to build up the mould in two pieces as shown by Fig. 40 which represents a midship mould. It will be noted that the mould is made in two pieces joined at the bottom by a piece and a cross piece at the top.

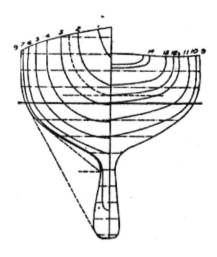

Fig. 34.—Body plan of 6-metre yacht design

The two sides can be cut out at one operation by fastening the two pieces together, having previously marked out the curved side, either by pricking through the section line on the full-size body plan or by making a tracing and sticking the paper to the mould. The cross sections on the body plan usually show the outside of the planking, but the mould has to be smaller by the thickness of the finished plank. Therefore, the cross piece at the top is made two-tenths of an inch less than the breadth of beam shown and a piece one-tenth inch is sawn off the centre line of the mould at B. The jogs or notches in the mould for the keel, the inwales and the lower one for the bilge stringer are now cut.

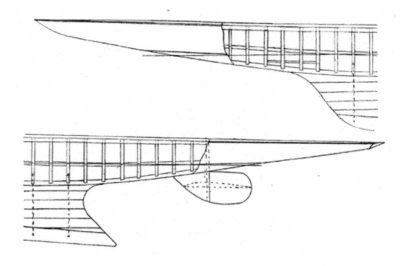

Fig. 35.—Sheer plan 10-rater, showing construction

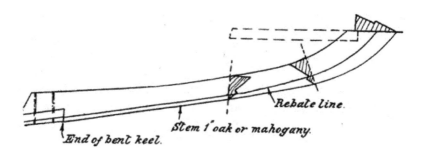

Fig. 36.—Sketch of stem

Just here a hint or two on the necessity of proper plans to work to. A full-size drawing of the body plan is an absolute necessity, while a full-size drawing of the sheer plan and the half deck plan will be most useful.

The moulds at the extreme ends may be made of single pieces of wood, but do not forget that the thickness of the planking must be taken off close to the curved edges.

With this particular method of construction it will be found better to build the mould upside down on a board or frame, the length of the moulds being prolonged to meet the datum line shown in the drawings. The moulds are then set up on the board, and it must be noticed that only the midship mould is set up dead over the line representing the position of the midship section. The moulds forward of the midship section are set up with their after edges on the station lines, while those aft of the mid-section are set up with their forward edges on the station line. This is to allow for bevelling the moulds which will be done later.

The building board is, of course, a little longer than the boat you are building, but it need not be wider than 6 in. and about 3/4 in. in thickness with two pieces of 3/4 in. stuff screwed to the underside running the full length of the board. The moulds are fastened to the board by means of pieces of 3/4 in. stuff nailed or screwed to them.

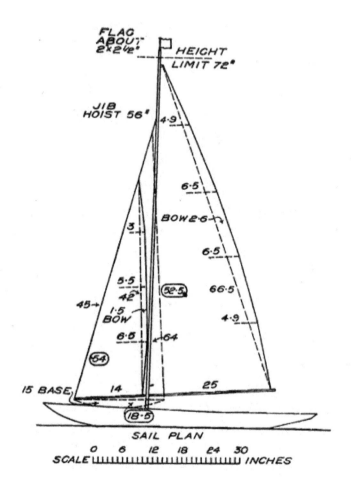

FLAG
ABOUT
2"x2½"

HEIGHT
LIMIT 72"

JIB
HOIST 56"

4·9

6·5

BOW 2·6

3

6·5

5·5

45→

42"

52·5

66·5

1·5
BOW

4·9

6·5

64

54

25

15 BASE

14

18·5

SAIL PLAN

SCALE

0   6   12   18   24   30

INCHES

Fig. 37.—Sail plan for 6-metre yacht (see Fig. 33)

Having set up the moulds the keel can now be made and
the rebate cut. This rebate, owing to the flatness of the floor of
the example given, can be partly cut with a rebate plane and
afterwards finished with a chisel and the notches or jogs for

the heels of the ribs also cut out. To get the correct spacing for the ribs the keel is bent round in the notches left for its reception in the moulds. The frames are spaced 2 in. apart, centre to centre, and there will therefore be one between each mould. The spacing is marked on the centreline drawn on the building board and squared up on to the keel. The frames being 1/4 in. X 1-10th in., the jogs for the heels of the ribs are, of course, the same width and depth and are cut in that portion of the keel rebate that will be covered by the lower strake of the planking.

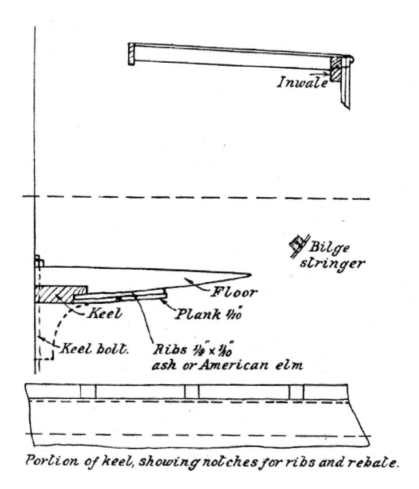

Portion of keel, showing notches for ribs and rebate.

Fig. 38.—Cross-section of 10-rater, showing constructional details

Note that a notch is to be cut also at each mould as a rib will later be filled in the space occupied by the moulds. The stem is also made from the drawing and placed up to a triangular section and the rebate cut. The sketch of the stem shows the approximate shape of the rebate at different points. The stem and keel are then fastened together by means of screws and glue, the glue being preferably such a glue as Test or other casein glue, and the stern transom made and fitted and finally the keel bent round over the moulds and temporarily secured. The inwale and the bilge stringers are also put in position, the inwale being secured at the ends by a triangular piece as shown. Then a number of battens of spruce or pine are taken and fitted round on top of the moulds. These battens will show where the moulds require bevelling, and before the battens are finally secured the bevelling is attended to. One batten is fitted at the sheer line and the others are spread about 1 in. apart all round the moulds. To get the correct spacing divide the distance round the curved sides of the mould from gunwale to keel by the number of battens and do the same at each mould. The battens are cut to fit in the stem rebate and are secured there by screws and also to the moulds and transom in the same way. The ribs are now fitted and the thin material will almost bend round cold, but if not very little steaming or soaking in hot water will be required. A rib is taken and passed between the sheer batten and the inwale and then bent round inside hard up against the battens with the end fitted into the jog cut for its reception in the keel rebate and the end is fastened with a small brad and glue. Fit all the ribs in a similar fashion, working from amidships to the ends securing the ribs to the inwale and, if they have been steamed, allowing them to dry. The planking can then be started, the garboard strakes on either side being first fitted after the batten next to the keel has been removed.

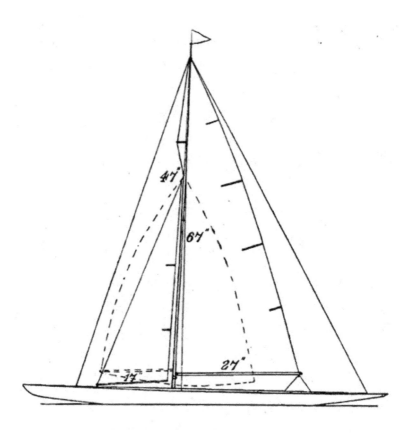

Fig. 39.—Sail plan of 10-rater

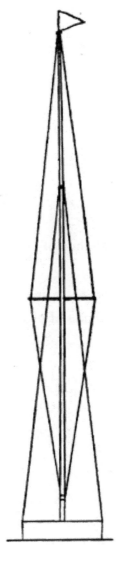

L.W.L

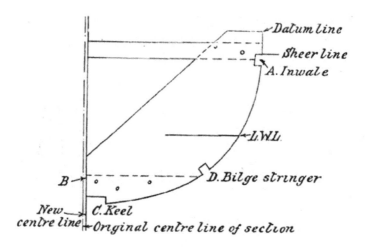

Fig. 40.—Method of making moulds

Distance between new centre line and original is equal to thickness of planking

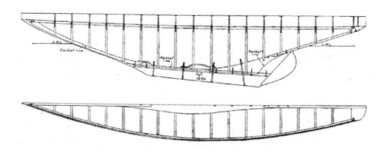

Fig. 41.—Diagram showing arrangement of keelson, mast steps, shadows of sections, and wood and lead keels in a 12-metre model

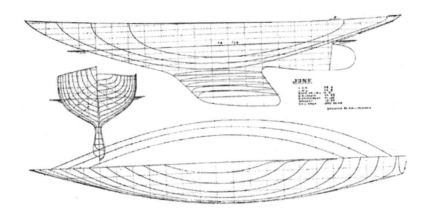

Fig. 42.—Sheer, half breath and body plans for "June," 6 metres

Fig. 43.—Arrangement of planking

In a boat of this type these strakes will be comparatively short. Note that all the ends of the planks will fit in the keel rebate and stem rebate and are fitted flat on top of the stern transom. The approximate width of the planks can be found in the same manner as was the spacing of the battens. The plank ends should be wide enough to allow of two fastenings, either No. 00 3-16ths in. brass screws or fine copper pins. The garboard strakes being fitted, the stem or gunwale strakes are cut and fitted, then the strake next to the garboard, then the one next the gunwale strake. The material for the planks can be either of pine or mahogany or cedar planed up to thickness of 1/8 in. The planks should be cut in pairs, both sides of the hull should be planked at the same time.

Fig. 44.—Planking at stern and transom

The hull when finished should be given several coats of linseed oil, which should be allowed to soak well into the planks. While this is drying, the deck work can be undertaken.

The deck beams of 1/4 in. X 3-16ths in. are spaced 4 in. apart, so that one will be fitted at every cross-section. The ends of the beams are dovetailed into the inwale, and where the mast and hatch openings occur the beams do not run right across but end on a fore and aft piece running between the two adjacent beams. If the deck is to be made in two pieces, a deck support 1/8 in. X 3/4 in. should be fitted below the deck, being let into the deck beams. If the rudder tube comes between two beams, a fore and aft centrepiece is fitted between the beams in front and behind the tube. The deck support answers the same purpose and the fore and aft piece is not necessary where this support is fitted. Before the deck is finally fixed, the whole of the inside should be given two coats of varnish and allowed to dry while the spars and other work are proceeded with.

The outside is also rubbed down, when the inside has dried. The deck should be of the same material as the planking. If this be mahogany or cedar the deck should be made of the same wood.

Finishing Touches

Finally the deck is fitted and the whole outside of the hull painted or varnished three coats. If the topsides are to be painted one colour and the underbody another the paint line must be laid off carefully. If you look at the drawing, Fig. 35, you will see that this is not parallel to the L.W.L. but rises at each end. To get this line laid off correctly will require careful work. The division between the two colours is sometimes made by what is called a "boot topping" or a narrow strip of a different colour painted between the two colours. When painting in the L.W.L., one colour, say the lighter of the two, is first laid on and allowed to dry, then the paint line is marked by a narrow strip of gummed paper stuck down on the paint already applied and the new coat, preferably the darker colour, is now put on and is painted over the gummed paper. When the gummed paper is removed a clean line is left behind.

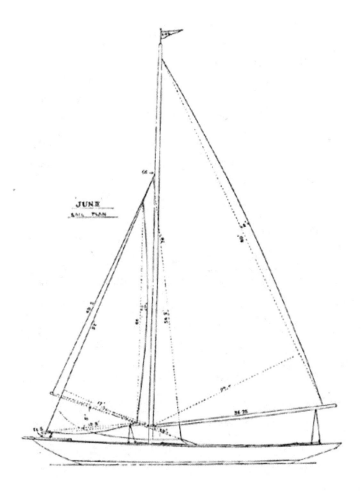

JUNE
SAIL PLAN

Fig. 45.—"A" class yacht "June" sail plan

The fin keel is built up as was the keel of the carved model, the fin being finally glued to the bent keel and secured by the keel bolts which run right through both lead and wood keels and are secured with nuts on the top of a floor.

CHAPTER VI

SPARS AND FITTINGS

WHILE aluminium masts are sometimes used for models, the other spars, owing to the necessity of tapering, are made of wood. The best way to make a tapering spar is first to get the wood, either spruce or pine, in square lengths to sizes required. The main boom and gaff should have one edge straight, the whole of the curve for taper being on the other side. For these first shoot one edge of the square stick straight and with a batten lay off the curve on face representing the amount of taper both on sides and face opposite the straight edge. Having planed down to these lines also plane off the corners, making the stick octagonal in section. If you have a concave plane, all these corners may again be removed, but from the octagonal stage it is a very simple matter to make the spar circular in section by glass-papering.

Coarse (i.e. No. 2) paper should be first used. Obtain from the oil shop a pennyworth of clear size, and, after melting down in an equal quantity of water, apply it to spars with a sponge. When dry the spars should be again glass-papered;

this time fine paper being used. Repeat the process three times, after which the markings for trimming sheets, which are done with an etching pen and Indian ink, may be made without fear of the ink running up the grain of the wood. The spars may be varnished almost immediately afterwards, one good coat being sufficient.

Hollow Spars

For those who have a fancy for excessive lightness in the rigging department, hollow spars are best made in the following manner:—

Two pieces of wood, a little thicker than half that of the finished spar, and the same breadth, are taken. After laying off the taper on face only at first, as in the case of solid spars, the wood is removed from the separate half spars by means of a gouge of suitable breadth; afterwards the hollow is smoothed by means of glass-paper wrapped around a small stick of suitable thickness.

The two halves may now be glued together, the wedge arrangement illustrated below being used to keep the spar straight during this process. When set, lay the taper on the sides and proceed as before as in the case of solid spars. Should your joints be good ones there is no need to whip the spars, but it will provide against trouble if this is done, silk being used for the purpose.

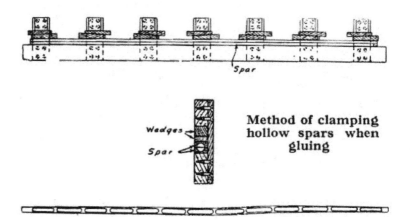

Method of clamping hollow spars when gluing

Fig. 46.—Half of spar (inside face)

It will be noticed that solid sections are left when gouging out, and these should be arranged to come into positions where screw-eyes are required.

Sails

For a model to put up a consistently good performance it is necessary that her sails shall retain their original shape. There are, of course, many methods of sail-making, but the following method is that by which the sails of every open race winner in the Metropolis for the last three years were made, so this should be good enough recommendation.

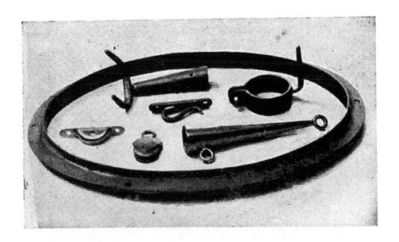

Fig. 47.—Hatch rim, gaff jaws, gooseneck, pulley, gunwale eye, spinnaker deck hook and jib-boom ferrule

The finest union silk should be used, as cotton sails are greatly affected by the atmosphere.

The material should be pinned down on a linoleum floor, or table, with drawing pins, just being pulled sufficiently to take out all creases.

The leech of the sail should be always parallel to the selvedge of the material.

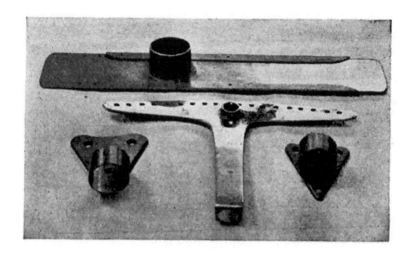

Fig. 48.—Mast slide, bowsprit fittings, and steering gear quadrant

If the sail has an outward bow, as is nearly always the case nowadays, the base must be set inside the selvedge sufficiently to allow for this, and also the amount of cloth required for them. In the mainsail set off the sail on the cloth just the same as if you were enlarging it to full size on paper. The edges of gaff and mainboom should be exactly straight, as the allowances that have to be made in large yacht sails owing to the spars bending are not required in a model. The luffs should have about 1/8 in. of hollow in every sail except the topsail.

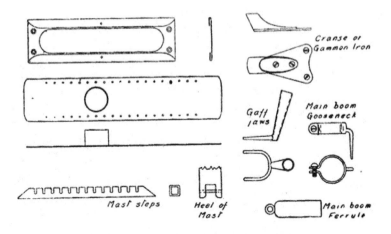

Fig. 49.—Various deck and spar fittings

Cut out the sails with a sharp penknife just outside the pencil lines. If your sewing machine has a hemmer, use it for the after leeches. The smallest possible hem is, of course, the best. Ascertain the size of your hemmer before cutting out the sail, as twice the width of the hem must be allowed for.

The secret of preventing the sails from stretching out of shape is to prevent the edges from being pulled. In order to ensure against this they are bound with a very strong material; pure linen tape, about 5/8 in. wide, for a 10-rater suit, and about 1/2 in. for smaller craft, is the best. This should be carefully folded down the centre and creased by rubbing over a sharp edge.

Until by practice the tape can be laid on direct, the

following method had better be followed: Tack the corner of the sail lightly inside the end of the binding, the raw edge of which should be folded in about 1/2 in., and drive a pin in the end to hold it down to the table. Take the binding in your right hand and just pull until it is taut. Place the edge of sail inside the binding, with your left hand, care being taken to get the edge of sail right into the fold, and just in its natural length. It can now be pinned all along this edge. Run a line of stitching (silk being preferable to cotton) along the inside edge of tape, afterwards binding the other edges, except the leeches, by the same method. In order to take all the creases out of the binding, another row of stitching around the extreme outside edge of the binding should be given.

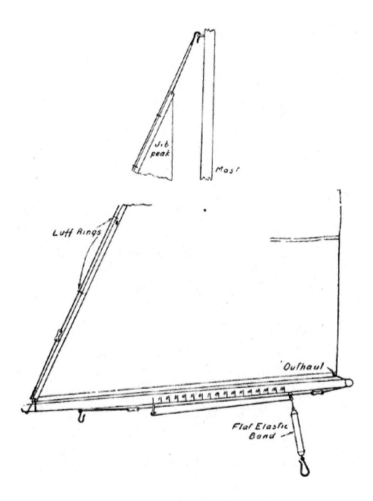

Fig. 50.—Details of rigging

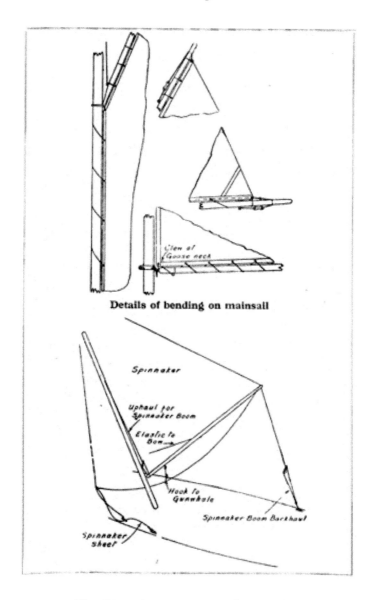

Details of bending on mainsail

Fig. 51.—Arrangement of spinnaker

If the sail edges of your spars are straight, and also the edges of sail, and if suitable tape is used to prevent the sail edges from stretching, the sails will remain as flat as when the material was pinned down on the drawing-board.

Eyelets should be let into the binding for lacing on to spars; the holes for these should not be punched out, but simply pierced with a sharp instrument, like a compositor's bodkin. Rings, as in rigging illustration, must be placed along the luff of jib for the jibstay to pass through. Crochet silk, or fishing silk, is better than cord for lacing.

In modern racing models it is usual to fit hooks to the luff and foot of a Bermudian (or triangular) mainsail. A wire jackline is fitted to the mast and boom passing through small screw-eyes which are spaced midway between the hooks on the sail. This is an improvement on the old method of lacing the sail to the spars.

CHAPTER VII

STEERING GEARS

ALTHOUGH the old pendulum and swing-weighted rudders are now things of the past, so far as racing models are concerned, there is only one steering gear that is worth writing upon. This gear was invented by Mr. G. Braine, of the M.Y.S.A., Kensington Gardens, and, although copied by nearly every model yachtsman throughout the Metropolis, few know its originator.

It is as perfect in its principle as a model steering gear could be, and in practice it has proved itself as good as a man at the helm.

When a model fitted with this gear does not perform properly when running or reaching, it is because it is either fitted badly, or, although the necessary parts may be present, their arrangement may be such as to spoil the whole idea.

This steering gear may be made strong and serviceable weighing about two ounces, and to this reason, and also its effectiveness, the present-day first-class models owe their success. Many models which were fitted with the old-fashioned rudders, depending upon the boat heeling to work them, although absolutely unmanageable down wind, became perfectly docile when fitted with this steering gear. Apart from its controlling ability, the lead which had to be left out of the keel for the swing rudders would cripple a light displacement boat like *XPDNC* for windward work, and also put her badly down by the stern when running—a feature which, although held by the ignorant to be a good thing, is not so.

On board a real yacht, the helmsman does not actually steer the boat. The sails are set at the most effective angle to the wind for the course required and the rudder is used simply to keep them drawing properly or for turning the boat on to the opposite tack.

The "Braine" Gear

As the tendency to get off the course comes with increasing speed, and as increasing speed is caused by increase of wind pressure upon the sails, what is more correct in principle than to make the very factor that tends to make the model deviate from her course work the rudder? While Mr. Braine was not the first one think of this idea, he was the first to invent a mechanical arrangement by which the angle of the rudder could be made to vary in exact proportion to the pressure of wind upon the sail.

With this steering gear you can give either weather helm or lee helm—excessive helm in a light wind and only slight amount as the wind hardens, or *vice versa*. It is possible by adjusting the tension of the elastic centring line to make the rudder keep straight until a given pressuré upon the mainsail is reached, or to go to a certain angle and no further at very little pressure; practically every variation may be obtained. In short, this gear may be adjusted to provide against any variation in the pressure of the wind; but no gear can provide against a change in the *direction* of the wind, as should this occur, the sails require retrimming to keep the original course.

The gear consists of a quadrant attached to rudder head, a pair of pulleys, a slide, and a piece of rubber cord. It is absolutely necessary that the rudder shall be perfectly free in its action: and for this purpose it is hung on a watch balance pintle. Only practice will enable the reader to use this gear in the proper manner, but the following will soon help him to grasp the principle:—

If the boat gets off the wind when the latter falls light, it is because the rudder does not come amidships under this condition; therefore the elastic requires tightening. Should the boat be inclined to keep straight while the wind is blowing fairly hard, but steers towards the wind as the latter drops light, the elastic is too tight, and must be slackened; at the same time the running line should be attached closer to the rudder head on the quadrant as the previous amount of leverage will be too great (when the wind blows harder) for the slacker elastic.

It will be seen that if with a certain tension of the elastic centring line, and pulling from a certain distance out on the quadrant, the happy combination is obtained to give the correct amount of helm for the varying pressures in the mainsail, an excessive amount of leverage on the quadrant obtained by moving the running line farther away from rudder head will cause the boat to run by the lee, i.e. turn away from the wind. A still further amount will finally cause her to gybe the mainsail on to the same side as the spinnaker.

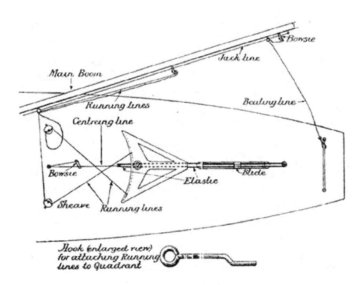

Fig. 52.—The "Braine" steering gear Universally used in the Metropolis and the Channel Islands

It will be noticed that there are two running lines that cross each other between the pulleys and the quadrant. As the mainboom goes over on to the other tack, it now being a shorter distance from point of attachment of the running lines to the original pulley than it is from the main boom to what is *now* the windward side one, the other line tautens and leaves the original one slack; therefore, if you arrange that on this tack the running line pulls from a point on the quadrant that gives an excessive amount of leverage over that which was required to keep the boat just straight on her course, the rudder will steer her way off the wind, and she will gybe back on to the original tack.

This short explanation should be sufficient to enable the model yachtsman to make effective use of the steering gear, and if the following is remembered very little trouble will be found.

If the model keeps off the wind too much when the latter falls light, the elastic centring line requires tightening, but if she is inclined to turn towards the wind under this condition, it requires slackening. If she is inclined to get too much off the wind as the latter increases in strength, less leverage is required, or *vice versa*.

Never attach running lines to the extreme ends of quadrant, and use the slide to check the angle.

Always make only slight alterations, as when once the

correct positions and tensions are found they will be correct for all time.

Don't blame the steering gear for not keeping the boat straight if your rudder is binding in the stock or tube.

Always see that when the pull is off both running lines the rudder comes back dead amidships.

Watch the sails to see if it was a change in the direction of the wind that put the boat off the course, and, if so, cure it by altering the angle and sets of the sail, and not by altering the steering gear.

As the speed of a yacht increases, the extra pressure on the leeward side of the rudder will be sufficient, and the extra amount of turning moment so created will obviate giving further angle of rudder.

When the wind is abeam the main sheet should be attached to the main horse, but slackened out sufficiently, so as not to prevent the other lines from working the rudder. It is then a simple matter, should the wind head the boat to the leeward shore to pull the main sheet up sufficiently on her arrival, not only to close haul the mainsail, but to cut out the weather helm at the same moment.

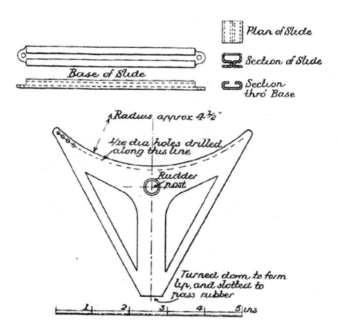

Plan of Slide
Section of Slide
Section thro' Base

Base of Slide

Radius approx 4½"

⅟₁₆ dia holes drilled along this line

Rudder post

Turned down to form lip, and slotted to pass rubber

Fig. 53.—Parts of the "Braine" steering gear

During recent years the practice of using jib-steering has increased. To fit this, in addition to the usual mainsail steering, lines are provided passing through pulleys and working in a similar manner off the jib-boom. This can be most efficacious under certain conditions, particularly in reaching winds. It requires care and experience to use it profitably, however, and in inexpert hands it may do more harm than good.

CHAPTER VIII

RACING SCHOONERS

IT has for years been generally accepted as law that the schooner rig is not so effective for windward work as that of a cutter, but many old theories have been proved false in model yachting of late, and the schooner *Prospero* proves conclusively that it is possible to design and build a schooner-rigged model that will hold her own with the best of the cutter fleet.

On her very first weather board, over a course of 280 yards, she gave the ten-rater *Valiant* 30 yards start and overhauled and passed her to weather in as true a sailing test as one could wish for. Those who saw the *Valiant* win the Cleveden Cup will realise that she is no mean trial horse. Of course, some allowance must be made for the difference in rating of these two boats, but the margin of superiority was more than the handicap demanded by Y.R.A. rules. Anyway, the schooner proved her ability to point as high as the sloop without loss of speed.

From a model sailing point of view, the schooner rig presents many advantages over the cutter. Firstly, nearly half of the total sail area is forward of the C.L.R. and either the gib, staysail or foresail may be used to steer with. By this, we do not mean that you should flatten any of them for the purpose of making the model find her head (if a boat is properly designed all the sails should have the same mean angle), but that a slight adjustment of any one of them would be more gradual in its effect than if the whole were in one sail.

The great trouble in a model schooner is to keep the gaff of the foresail aboard. This sail being high and narrow has a tendency to swing off unless very little sheet is given, in which case it jams on the horse, and more often than not stops on the weather side when the boat is put about. It is totally wrong in principle to sheet any sail from amidships. The manner in which this trouble was avoided was by means of a stay lead from a point 1 1/2 in. below the gooseneck to the middle of foresail boom, and adjustable with a bowser. This, while serving its purpose, does not prevent the sail swinging.

"Vices" and Their Effects

Before dealing with this boat as a schooner, it would be well to point out the various vices that it is possible for a yacht to possess which detract from her straight sailing, and to analyse the particular effect that each of these vices has upon the performance, irrespective of any particular form of rig. These vices, being in the hull, cannot possibly be eliminated by alteration either of proportion of headsail to mainsail, or the position of the whole over the hull.

If a yacht's hull is possessed of a feature which gives (in spite of her being bilateral when upright) a natural weather helm when heeled, and in motion, the shifting back of the sails will not cure it. You may overpower this force by so doing, but in all probability the rig will be so far back that as soon as she meets a lighter wind and becomes more or less upright and slowed down, this natural weather helm has disappeared, and the model will go into irons. The rig being then too far aft for her to pay off, and being unable again to develop that weather helm that she obtained from the motion given her at the start of the board, she will remain in irons.

Therefore, if we can eliminate those features that tend to steer the boat towards the direction in which she is heeled, we shall have solved the trouble of running off the wind. For these arguments to be consistent, to overdo the cure of these features will be to create the very opposite effect—that is, a tendency to sail away from the direction in which the yacht is heeled. Experiments carried out by pushing models possessed of this vice when artificially heeled to varying angles in smooth water and minus their rigs have proved these contentions true.

It will be seen why a model that holds a good wind in light airs may run off as soon as the speed increases, and why another that cannot look at the wind when it is light will go well under it in a stiff breeze.

Should the after-body be harder to drag than the forebody is to drive, the resolved centre of resistance to forward motion will travel slowly aft. This is proved by the fact that in the case of a large yacht that carries her helm dead amidships when going to windward, she requires lee helm to stop her running off if towing another boat. Another feature that will have the same effect is when the fin, or, in other words, the centre of the area of the underwater vertical plane, is too far back. This was the case in the Boston America cup defender *Independence*, and also *Constitution*. In light winds these boats could point just as high as the *Columbia*, but as soon as the wind increased and caused the yachts to heel over they demanded lee hélm to keep them pointing, consequently sliding bodily away to leeward. There is yet another feature that has become very prominent, especially in metre models, which, perhaps, is more serious still in producing the effect of broad-reaching when close-hauled; and this is converging stream lines in the after garboard—a matter that would take too much space to deal with fully in this volume. It is sufficient to say here that this is a question dealing with the proportion of the fin or keel that should be included in the calculation of the displacement curve.

The very first essential in a yacht's design is that her fore and aft proportions shall be so arranged that at each and every angle of heel the imaginary line joining the water line ending amidships remains parallel to the surface of water, that is, assuming the latter to be more or less smooth

TABLE OF OFFSETS, SCHOONER *PROSPERO.*

	Pro-file	Deck sheer	Heights and Depths Buttock Lines					Water Line. Half Breadths in Inches and Decimals											
			5	4	3	2	1	L	K	J	H	G	F	E	D	C	B	A	Deck
Bow	4.6	4.6					4.4											0.27	1.9
1	1.9	4.4					1.6									0.12	1.75	2.7
2	1.0	4.2					0.7								1.33	1.35	2.6	3.45
3	0.4	4.0		1.35	1.35	1.35	0.65							0.8	2.25	2.37	3.45	4.0
4	0.15	3.8		0.2	0.2	0.4	0.33						1.2	2.64	3.67	3.25	4.0	4.6
5	0.67	3.6		0.25	0.27	0.27	1.5				0.2	0.35	2.9	3.78	4.4	4.0	4.6	5.1
6	1.2	3.48	1.1	0.48	0.46	0.82	1.55		0.4	0.43	0.6	1.0	3.8	4.5	5.0	4.6	5.1	5.52
7	1.8	3.2	0.45	0.9	0.97	1.85	1.9	0.7	0.65	0.35	0.5	0.67	1.7	4.3	5.02	5.4	5.1	5.8
8	2.7	3.1	0.65	1.18	1.31	1.65	2.0	0.6	0.5	0.55	0.67	0.5	2.0	4.57	5.37	5.87	5.52	5.95
9	4.8	3.2	0.7	1.3	1.57	1.9	2.35	0.25	0.1	0.32	0.5	0.15	1.87	4.6	5.35	5.9	5.8	6.0
10	6.7	2.98	0.6	1.15	1.5	2.0	2.5				0.15		1.34	4.4	3.6	5.58	5.95	5.92
11	8.0	2.83	0.2	0.9	1.2	1.8	2.43					0.1	0.6	3.72	5.53	5.7	6.0	5.8
12	8.8	2.7	1.15	0.5	0.83	1.47	2.15				0.1	0.1	0.2	2.15	4.8	5.4	5.92	5.52
13	9.0	2.68		0.7	0.88	1.03	1.77				0.1	0.1	0.1	0.1	3.97	4.3	5.8	5.15
14	3.35	2.65		1.8	1.6	0.65	1.27								1.8	2.27	5.52	4.67
15	4.0	2.65				0.65	0.7										5.15	4.1
16	4.4	2.66				1.26	0.5										4.67	3.35
17	0.18	2.7				1.9	1.1										4.1	2.27
18	0.4	2.72					1.7										3.35	2.7
19	1.0	2.75					2.3										2.27	1.87
20	1.6																	
Transom	2.83	2.83																

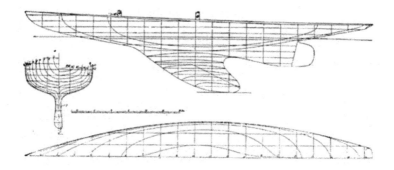

Fig. 54.—The lines of "Prospero"

Fig. 55.—"Prospero" "Wind abeam"

Should, on heeling, the boat stoop by the head (known as boring), the leading edge of the fin or centreplate will at once try to cut its way downwards. The buoyancy of the yacht resisting this, we have an inclined surface being dragged through the water in a direction other than parallel to its natural axis, producing a great resistance to forward motion, and dragging the resolved centre of resistance forward. All yachts that bore, tend to gripe up into the wind as their speed increases. In the same manner if a yacht squats by the stern when heeled, the after-body becomes a drag upon the whole; and she will run off the wind, because the resolved centre of the resistance to forward motion of the new shape that is immersed is then farther aft in relation to the C.E. of sails than when upright. It will thus be seen that it would be more detrimental to a yacht's performance if her entrance and delivery were out of harmony with each other, than if the fore-body or after-body were reduced to correspond to the speed of the slower.

As it is seen that certain features create different effects, it is quite possible to use one of these features to counteract another of opposite effect. Many inferior hulls have been made to sail straight by this means, but these vices are fighting against each other, and, of course, produce a great loss of speed, leeway resulting.

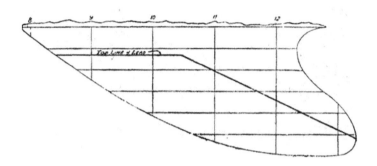

Fig. 56.—Diagram showing line of lead keel of schooner yacht "Prospero." Scale: 3 in. = 1 ft.

Another serious feature is when the axis of the new shape that is immersed when heeled becomes out of parallel with the original amidships line. You then have your hull wanting to point either a closer wind than the fin, if the fore-body is too fine, or *vice versa* if the after-body is too fine.

It may be asked how are we to arrange that the centre of forward resistance of the hull will remain in a fixed position. As a matter of fact, it is not desirable that it should remain exactly so, but should move forward and keep a position relative to the centre of effort of the sails, which, as has long been proved, moves forward in proportion to the speed at which the wind passes across them. As by heeling the boat we increase her length more aft than forward, this feature is used to advantage and by placing the largest immersed section slightly behind the middle of the L.W.L. it is arranged that it becomes

131

exactly amidships when heeled to the maximum sailing angle. It thus causes the displacement curve which, when upright, was slightly shorter abaft the greatest section, to become of equal length either side of its highest point, and if the sections are in character throughout the hull it will maintain the same graduation. In order that the yacht shall use her overhangs it is necessary that they shall be of correct proportionate buoyancy to that part of the hull which will be immersed when heeled. Overhangs that are simply licked by the bow and stern waves are more detrimental than useful. In order to remove the reserve buoyancy amidships as much as possible, and to increase the call upon the overhangs, some designers tumble home the topsides, but the very slight decrease of sectional area is so small that it is not worth much, as not only does it flatten the streamlines and topside diagonals, but it makes the boat lifeless when before the wind.

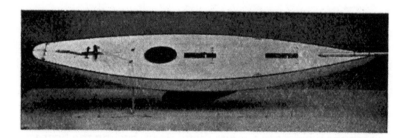

Fig. 57.—Deck view, showing arrangement of fittings

As all these features have to be taken into consideration

irrespective of rig, and are concerned in the hull alone, the proportion of driving sail to pulling sail should not have any influence on hull design, providing the latter is free from any of the before-mentioned vices, which tend to steer her. In other words, if the hull of its own accord does not develop a tendency to sail in a circle when pushed in smooth water artificially heeled without her sails on, it is a simple matter to get a suitable sail plan and its correct position of C.E. over the hull. A sail plan, in which the mainsail forms a large proportion of the whole, will demand the centre of effort farther forward of the C.L.R. than if the proportions were more equal. As the ability to point high in light winds practically depends upon the closeness of the C.E. to the C.L.R., it is only necessary to design a boat that will carry a large proportion of headsail to windward in a strong wind to ensure her holding a good wind when it falls light. It is a fallacy to believe that a yacht will not go to windward under headsail alone, in proof of which it may be stated that a race sailed by the South Coast One Design Class, in which three out of five starters carried staysail alone, the other two having reefed mainsails, the latter two finished behind the other three, and, curiously enough, it was on the windward legs that the former made their gain.

Fig. 58.—Close racing ("A" class): "Gertrude" (winner, International Race, 1927) leading "Frolic"

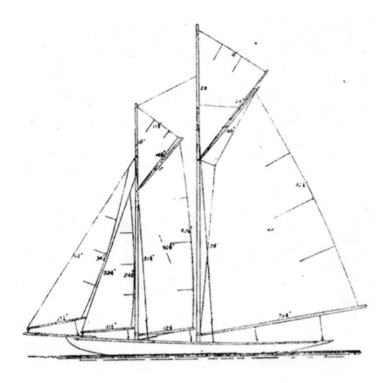

Fig. 59.—Sail plan of schooner "Prospero"

Fig. 60.—"Prospero"

As it will be seen from the foregoing statements that in order to carry a large proportion of headsail to windward it is absolutely necessary that every vice tending to give the hull artificial weather helm must be eliminated, it is patent that in a hull that is to be a schooner (which of all rigs has the largest proportion of headsail) these vices would be fatal.

The hull of this model is built of pine, is finished in white topsides and malachite under-body, and all the fittings are of brass, nickel-plated. All the spars are of pine, except the masts and bowsprit, which are 26-gauge aluminium tube. The hull is 61 1/2 in. over all, 41 in. on the load water line. It will be noticed that the actual L.W.L. comes between those shown in the design. This was done for economy and for no other reason. She has sails of the finest union silk, and is fitted with the steering gear invented by Mr. G. Braine, of the Model Yacht Sailing Association, which piece of mechanism is, perhaps, the greatest of all model yachting inventions. It is used universally in the Metropolitan area, and even in Guernsey the writer found it fitted to his opponent's boat on his visit there some time ago for the Channel Isles Championship, much to his surprise and very nearly to his cost.

Prospero's total displacement is 20 lb., and she has 12.5 lb. of lead in her keel which is brass shod, and is bolted right through the fin with 10-gauge motor-cycle spokes.

The details of fittings are apparent from the drawings and photographs, and nothing that could be done to ensure success was neglected. It is remarkable with what quickness she fills again after coming about on the gye, but this is due to the large amount of headsail that spills when she comes into the wind, and the great distance the C.E. of the mainsail is behind the C.L.R.

The photos of schooner are by Mr. G. Barratt.

CHAPTER IX

TUNING UP AND SAILING

THE chapter upon the schooner *Prospero* will give the reader a fair idea of cause and effect. As was remarked therein, speed and steadiness go hand in hand, provided the latter is obtained by the natural harmony of the whole model, and not by brute force, such as a very long keel or double fins.

Although a double-fin boat will no doubt beat an erratic model, she would stand little chance against a boat like *XPDNC* in a dead heat to windward, as, being slow to turn, they do not take advantage of a free puff of wind, and are slow to fill away should the wind head them.

Although in the latter case they may keep a higher weather position, the other kind of boat would have moved forward more than sufficient to compensate for it.

In order to be successful in model yacht racing it is necessary to get your boat tuned up to such a pitch that any alteration of trim of sails gives a direction in proportionate difference.

For instance, a boat is totally wrong somewhere if a quarter of an inch more mainsheet causes her to change her course from beating to reaching, and yet this is the case with quite a number of craft.

However, a slight alteration in the fore and aft trim will oft-times have considerable effect upon the performance of a model.

It was not intended to deal with elements of yacht design in this volume, but the following is necessary for the beginner to comprehend the various forces that come into play as the boat increases speed.

The point known as the centre of lateral resistance (C.L.R.) is the spot in the underwater vertical plane of the boat at which the centre of resistance to sideways movement is concentrated when at rest. This spot is the point about which the model would revolve when afloat, and not travelling fore and aft, but directly a yacht starts to travel forward this centre is likely to alter its fore and aft position.

As the straight and steady sailing of any yacht, whether model or manned, depends upon the centre of the sail plan keeping in a certain position relative to the C.LR. at all speeds, it will be seen that the endeavour of the yachtsman is to contrive to keep these centres from altering their relative positions. In the case of a large yacht the crew act as shifting ballast and by altering their position at varying angles of heeling contrive to counteract any tendency of the C.L.R. to alter its original position.

As the model yachtsman has no such facilities for maintaining the fore and aft trim of his boat, it is first necessary for her to do it by her natural harmony of hull.

Many model yacht hulls are of such formation that no alteration of trim, position of sails or fin will allow them to keep their sails drawing at a consistent angle to the wind at every angle of heel.

It is not so much essential that the sails should be set at a certain angle to the amidships line of hull as it is that the bow should naturally fall away from the wind into such position that the sails draw at the most effective angle to the *wind*.

Should your boat have a tendency to come into the wind when the latter lightens in strength, your sail plan requires moving forward, or aft if the opposite is the case. It may be, however, that she will sail kindly enough until the wind is strong enough to press her over to a certain angle, when she may suddenly screw up to windward and the sails shake, in which case the trimming of her slightly by the stern will probably eradicate this. A small piece of lead fixed upon the counter should be experimented with, afterwards fixing it below deck. The sail plan will, however, require to be moved slightly aft as you have now moved the underwater body farther aft in relation to the position of the rig.

All this, of course, must necessarily be known in order to

correct the wayward tendencies of your craft; for the secret of success in racing is to provide against the little things that happen and spoil the performance momentarily, oft-times just making the difference between winning and losing.

If, when racing, it is obvious that the courses are a dead beat to windward, and a run back before the wind, you would, of course, trim your boat to do her best performance under these conditions, the trim for which, by practice, you should have previously ascertained, but, as often happens, the wind does not always keep true. In races sailed under the M.Y.A. tournament system, in which each competitor has two courses with each of his opponents, separately, it is at once apparent that it is of little use winning one board by half the length of the course and losing another by 6 in., as there is no credit given for the distance that you cross the finishing line in front of your opponent. It therefore does not pay to take risks in order to win a course by a large margin.

The Other Man's Boat

If you have previously raced with your opponents you will have a fair idea of the relative merits of their boats as compared with your own. Anyway, you should watch them, and judge from their performances in their heats previous to meeting you.

Should you have noticed, for instance, that your next opponent is closer winded than you have reason to believe your boat is, don't try to make your boat point a higher wind than you have found her to be capable of doing, as your chance of defeating him to windward depends upon your being able to forereach him sufficiently to enable you to make up for the greater distance your model will have to travel.

It is quite likely, too, that the wind may free sufficiently to allow you to just fetch the winning line without tacking, and the fact that your opponent finishes at the weather end of the line, while you finish to leeward, will help him little if he crosses only a foot behind you.

By the same argument if you are aware that your boat is closer winded than your opponent's, sail a slightly freer wind, as you are sure to outfoot him by doing so; and even if you do get headed away, so also will he.

On a squally day it is often noticeable that the wind is either freeing or heading during the hard puffs. To be correct in principle, the angle of set of the sails should be altered; but as this is not possible on a model the steering gear must be brought into play to counteract the alteration in the direction of the wind during the squalls. This is easily possible if the Braine steering gear is used correctly. You would, of course, have a very tight centring line, if the squalls are coming free, and if the wind heads the squalls, check the rudder by means of the pinrack, so that the boat gets a little less helm than would have been necessary had the angle of the wind not altered, in which case the boat will luff and keep on the course. As at low speeds the shape of a boat has far less effect upon her speed than under conditions when high speeds are obtainable, it is often the case that an owner is at a loss to know why a boat that is inferior to him in a breeze can outsail him when practically drifting.

This is because his boat either does not lie naturally at that angle to the wind which enables the sails to draw properly, or else he has not enough sail area in proportion to the weight of the boat. It may only require a few square inches more to overcome inertia and set the mass in motion, but if the necessary sail is there, the boat will be able to maintain momentum often when apparently there is no wind whatever.

It does not pay, however, to have a boat that is superlative under these conditions if it is gained at the expense of good performance in harder winds, as a race cannot be sailed under the tournament system if you are the only boat that can cover the course.

Many yachtsmen pay tremendous attention to wetted surface, but as the resistance from skin friction is only about 1 per cent. of the total resistance, and that in boats of the same rating the wetted area cannot be made to vary greatly unless the power of the vessel is reduced by curtailing beam or draught it may, if too much importance is attached to it, cause the designer to neglect far more important features.

Fig. 61.—"Defiance," winner International Race, 1926. Capt. F. W. Lazell, Forest Gate M.Y.C.

Finally, in sailing, do not make the model do anything that you could not make her do if you were aboard, and always sail keenly, as even though you are not leading on points you must always remember that the man whose boat is leading is depending upon you beating his opponents as well as defeating them himself.

In a run before the wind or a broad reach, unless your

opponent is obviously in error by not carrying a spinnaker, you should do likewise, unless you know his boat is faster than yours, and your only chance is by taking advantage of that sail and trusting to the wind not heading during the course.

By watching the boats that have started in previous heats, you can judge fairly well the direction of the wind, and act accordingly.

When setting the spinnaker care should be taken that it is set in such manner that the mainsail will spill the wind first, should a heading puff of wind strike her.

Great care should be taken to see that the gaff swings easily at the jaws, and rather have the peak of the mainsail a little too low than over peaked, as the latter often makes the boat fidgety and inclined to drive her up into the eye of the wind.

The principle upon which the gye is used is either for ensuring the boat keeping on the tack upon which she started, or to make her change tack after sailing a certain distance. It consists of an elastic cord about 9 in. in length with a length of line sufficient to extend it until it will reach from a point upon the deck rail about opposite the middle of the mainboom to the after end of the latter, a bowser being used to adjust the length.

If the boat is tuned up to that pitch of windward work that a slightly closer hauling of the mainsail will make her jib shake, the influence of the gye when the model is put off upon the tack in which it comes into play will have the effect of closer hauling the mainsail upon this tack.

While the jib remains full of wind, however, the pressure of the wind upon the mainsail should be able completely to stretch the gye until the mainsail pulls properly upon the mainsheet, but the presence of the gye will cause the model to come into the wind slowly, and at the moment the jib shakes it will be able to assert itself and by pulling the mainsail over to windward cause the hull to revolve until the jib falls upon the other tack. The gye will then be dormant until the boat comes ashore; that is, unless a contrary puff of wind should strike her. A rigid gye is wrong in principle, as there is no reason why the mainsail should be badly set upon the off-shore tack.

When in racing your boat comes to shore outside the finishing flags, don't make too violent an alteration, as perhaps you are only at a slight angle off the course.

Fig. 62.—Crowds watching International Races at Gosport.

When the course is a run or a reach, always keep nearer to the leeward shore in preference to the windward as it is easier to draw off the former than bear away from the latter; also the wind is generally stronger on the leeward shore.

Never push violently at the start as the water disturbance so caused will do you more harm than good.

Rules and Their Observance

As in large yacht sailing various rules have been formed to avoid accidents, and also give proper understanding between the skippers of adjacent vessels, so in model racing laws have been made to regulate the sailing.

When possible, the course is arranged so that the wind blows dead down, giving a beat to windward one way and a run with a spinnaker back again, in which case it is the general rule to give 3 points for winning the windward heats and 2 for winning leeward ones.

The uninitiated onlooker is often unable to understand how a race is being carried out, as he sees the boats coming up the course in pairs.

It is obvious that if there were eight or ten entries in a race, and all started together, apart from the risk of a general mix up, the boat that had the windward position would be at a decided advantage, whilst the leeward boats would be practically out of it before the race commenced. Therefore, in order to give every boat a fair chance, the races are sailed either on the M.Y.A. tournament system or else on the knock-out principle.

In the former each boat meets all the other competitors in a course to windward, and a course to leeward. Points are gained for each course, and at the finish the boat having won the greatest number of points is the winner of the race.

In the knock-out system the boats are drawn in pairs, and have a certain number of courses against each other.

The winners in the first round go into the second, and so on, until only two boats remain to form the final round, the winner of this being the winner of the race.

The latter system is advisable when a very large entry is received. When only three entries are obtained, they start all together, and sail a certain number of courses, each having the weather berth in turn.

GENERAL SAILING RULES.—On entering a club you will be supplied with a book of sailing rules, which are framed with the object of regulating the racing in such manner that the boats must be made to cover the course by use of the wind and sails only.

It always pays to sail fairly, but of course occasions arise when, owing to a risk of fouling, a rule must be made to determine which boat shall have the right of way.

The rule is for the boat that is going to be put off shore in the beat to windward either to wait, if there is a risk of fouling an incoming boat, or, if the owner risks it, to forfeit the points should a foul occur.

On running or reaching boards a boat must be retrimmed by alteration to sails or steering gear should she come ashore outside the winning line. This is intended to be a penalty for being off the course and before the present-day arrangements of sheets and rudders certainly was so, but many boats seem to gain speed during this process.

There must be little satisfaction, however, in winning other than by superior speed.

In making an off-shore tack on the gye the head of the boat must be turned off the wind sufficiently to make the headsail fill, disqualification being the penalty for not doing so.

Finally, if you race, let it be for the sport, for, if the accumulation of plate alone be your object, remember that yacht racing is a slow and expensive method of attaining your end.

CHAPTER X

NOTES ON SAILING FOR BEGINNERS

THE art of sailing a model consists in so setting the sails—or "trimming" them, as the nautical term is—that she will continue to sail along the course decided upon by the yachtsman with as small a deviation as possible and in a speedy manner. The trim of the sails will be different according to whether the boat is to sail against the wind (which is called "beating to windward"), with the wind (which is called "scudding"), or with the wind sideways (which is "reaching"). These are the principal divisions of sailing; but there is another case, in which the boat may be sailing with the wind blowing midway between one of the sides and the stern, so that it sweeps from one of the corners of the stern across the deck. This is called "three-quarter sailing" or "three-quarter reaching," or "a quartering wind." Fig. 70, Q, shows the direction of the wind and the course of a yacht sailing under these conditions. Whilst a yacht will continue for any distance on a reach, or scudding before the wind, it is not possible for her to sail directly against the wind, except for the very short distance her momentum may carry her. When sailing against a wind

152

the yachtsman must therefore make a compromise, and dodge the wind, as it were, by sailing as near dead against it as his boat will go. A cutter will move against a wind which is blowing at a very small angle to the point of her bowsprit. In this way she follows a limited course which, whilst not being directly against the wind, yet takes the yacht a certain distance in the direction from which the wind is blowing. As soon as she reaches the limit of her course the yacht's bows are turned through a small angle so as to bring the wind on the other side of the vessel, and a second course is followed. These courses are repeated each time, gaining so much distance to windward until the boat arrives at its destination. This dodging about is called "tacking." Fig. 63 shows a model yacht tacking to windward from B to C; she starts at B, and arrives against the wind at C by means of three tacks as shown by the dotted lines. Each time she touches the shore at A, A she is "put about," as it is termed, upon a new tack. The left-hand side of a ship viewed from the stern is called the "port" side, and the right-hand is called the "starboard" side. A yacht sailing with the wind blowing anywhere on her port side is said to be on the port tack; if the wind is blowing on her starboard side she is on the starboard tack. From this explanation it will be seen that Fig. 64 (A) shows an impossible case, Fig. 63 being the method actually adopted in sailing to windward.

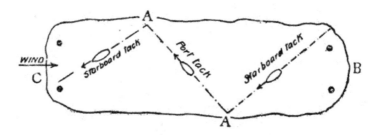

Fig. 63.—Tacking to windward

The sails in front of the mast which are nearest to the stem of the yacht act so as to turn the bows in the direction of the arrow *b*, Fig. 65 (the sails are represented by thick black lines), and the sail or sails behind (or "abaft," as the nautical term is) the mast turn the bows in the direction of the arrow *a*, the boat revolving upon the centre of the mast like a weather cock upon its pivot. If there is more than one mast all the sails carried abaft the mainmast act to turn the boat in the direction of *a*; and this rule holds good with the wind in all positions relatively to the boat. The art of sailing thus largely depends upon a knowledge of so balancing these two effects that the boat will move in a straight line. In order to effect this, the sails are set at a greater or less angle to the centre line of the boat. The less the angle which a sail makes with the centre line the greater is its power to determine in which direction the boat will steer; the more you slacken out the jib and foresail, or the smaller you make these sails, the less will be their power to turn the boat towards *b*; conversely, the larger they are, or the more tightly they are pulled in, the greater will be their power. With the mainsail and all others abaft the mainmast, the more you slacken them out and the smaller they are the less will be their power to turn the boat in the direction of a. The influence of a sail upon the speed of the boat, however, increases with the angle which it makes with the centre line of the hull; the more you slacken out a sail the more it will help the boat along. The two conditions, therefore, interfere with one another to a more or less extent, and the trimming of the sails becomes a compromise. It is by this that the more skilful yachtsman wins the race over a less experienced or talented competitor, given equal luck, as the wind may vary in strength or direction, or in both, to an extent sufficient to upset the calculations relied upon. As a general rule, sail your boat as free as possible—that is, with the sails as slack as you can—so long as she keeps a good course. Do not overload her with canvas, as the nearer she sails to an upright position the faster she will go with a given force of wind.

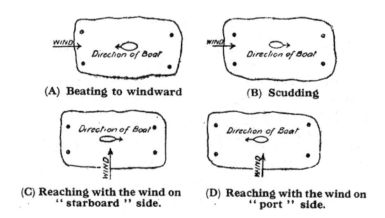

(A) Beating to windward   (B) Scudding

(C) Reaching with the wind on " starboard " side.   (D) Reaching with the wind on " port " side.

Fig. 64.

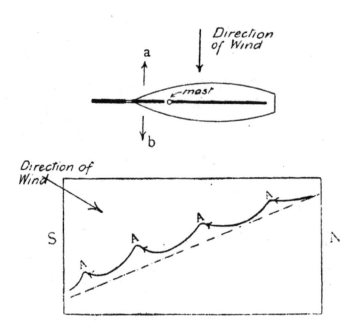

Fig. 65. Effect of wind pressure on the sails.

RUDDERS.—As already mentioned, it is not possible to depend entirely upon the trim of the sails alone to keep a model yacht upon a given course, as the wind always varies in strength; so that, if the sails are in balance for one moment, they are out of balance the next. The sails abaft the mainmast overpower the sails before it when the wind increases, with the result that the bows of the boat are repeatedly turned in the direction of *a*, Fig. 65 (of course, with the wind on the other side the direction would be reversed; it is always towards the direction from which the wind is blowing). Some form of self-acting rudder is therefore generally used to counteract this tendency to "screw," or "luff into the wind," as it is called. Fig. 65 is a diagram of the course of a yacht reaching from the end N of a pond to the other end S. The dotted line shows the straight course which she ought to follow; the full line shows the effect of repeated puffs of wind in making her deviate to the points A at each puff. She will also lose speed and almost come to a standstill at each point, because as the wind dies away the headsails may re-assert themselves and pull the bow round towards the proper course, the yacht meanwhile having lost her speed, as she will be pointing almost directly against the wind. She may even turn completely round, and make a similar course back to the starting point, as in Fig. 67. There is also the risk that she will be taken aback when pointing directly against the wind—that is, the wind will force her backwards stern first for some distance (see Fig. 68), until she manages to shake free and get round on one tack or the other. The dotted line B shows the course in which she would be driven under these conditions. When scudding before the wind the headsails have very little influence, with the result that it is not practicable to sail a model dead before the wind without a self-acting rudder. She will turn round towards the wind as the after sails have complete control. By the use of a self-acting rudder the erratic movements shown in Figs. 65 and 68 can be prevented, and the boat kept steadily on her course. The action of the rudder is such that every time the boat leans over in the puffs to luff up into the wind the weight of the rudder causes it to swing out and prevents her from leaving her course. As a different power of rudder is required according to the course which the boat is sailing, the weight must be adjustable if the same rudder is used or several rudders can be used of different weights. This is one of the secrets why many of the toyshop boats, and those made by anyone who does not know anything about model yacht sailing, do not sail well or keep to a definite course.

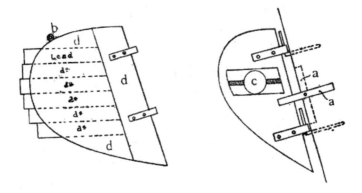

Fig. 66.—Swing rudders.

SCUDDING BEFORE THE WIND.—For this course put on the heaviest rudder, or the weight on a loaded tiller to its position of greatest power; slack out all the sails abaft the foremast as much as they will go, so that the booms stand almost at right angles with the centre line of the boat. If a cutter or yawl, and the wind is light, rig up the spinnaker. The headsails may be left slack or not; theoretically, they should be as slack as possible, but they do scarcely any work in a model when scudding, and it does not usually make any appreciable difference whether they are tight or slack. Fig. 69 shows the position of the booms when scudding in (A) a schooner, and (B) a yawl "scudding goose winged," as it is called, (C) a cutter with spinnaker set, (D) a two-masted lugger with balanced lugs. If the wind is blowing strong with heavy puffs, it may be well to take in topsails so as to relieve the boat and prevent her from plunging her bows under water. It depends, however, upon the qualities of the particular boat. A properly made model, if correctly trimmed and fitted with suitable rudder, will sail true and straight dead before the wind.

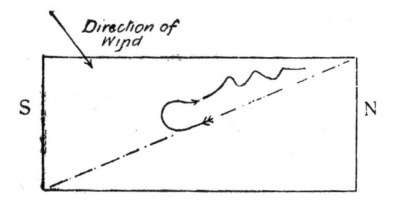

Fig. 67. A complete turn round.

REACHING.—For this put on a medium rudder, rather light than heavy (in a set of four detachable rudders, the lightest but one); with a weighted tiller put the weight at about mid position. Headsails should be pulled in fairly tight, and aft-sails should be slack, but not so slack as for scudding. Fig. 70 is a diagram of a schooner reaching; the thick black lines are the booms of the sails. When the wind is very light a spinnaker jib may be set (or "balloon jib," as it is also called), or a "jib topsail" in light or moderate breezes. If the wind is not directly abeam, but comes off the stern quarter, such as indicated by arrow (Q) in Fig. 70, then the next heavier rudder, or its equivalent in the weighted tiller, may be required, and the sails slackened out rather more than before. The boat is then said to be sailing free on the starboard tack. If the wind is in the direction of the arrow R, the jib and foresail may require slackening a trifle less, and the after sails pulled in rather more than when sailing with the wind in direction (A). A lighter rudder still would be used as the course is getting near beating to windward, and the yacht is said to be "close hauled to the starboard tack"; but she would be still reaching, as you would not desire to work up into the wind.

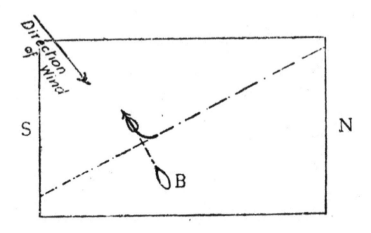

Fig. 68. Effect of being taken aback.

BEATING TO WINDWARD.—If a rudder is used at all it should be a very light one, just to keep the boat steady; but this is just the condition of sailing when a model can dispense with a rudder. It depends upon the characteristics of the particular yacht, which can only be found out by experience. A jib topsail should not be used, and, if the wind is fairly strong a smaller jib should be set than that used for reaching. The jib and foresail should be slackened out, and the aft-sails pulled in tight, but not too tightly. Fig. 71 is a diagram of a cutter beating to windward on the port tack; she will have to pay off to starboard a bit before her sails begin to fill.

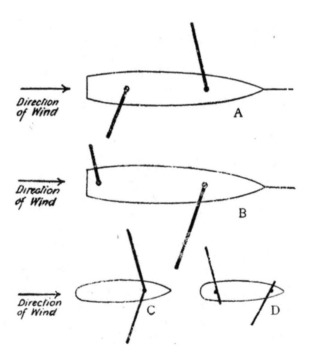

Fig. 69. Position of booms when scudding.

GENERAL HINTS ON SAILING AND RACING.—
The amount of sail to carry should depend upon the weather.
It is bad to try to force a yacht to carry more canvas than
she can comfortably sail under. If she has too much she will
heel over and drag her sails in the water, and also drift to
leeward when beating to windward. When sailing a new boat
her best trim for various points of sailing and force of wind
must be found by careful experiment. Always sail your boat
with sheets as slack as she will take them whilst keeping to her
course, as she will move faster than if the sheets are strained
in tight. When beating to windward you should try to keep
her well on the move; rather set a smaller jib or foresail than
have to force your boat by straining in the mainsail to the
last hole. Aim rather at moving fast upon an easy series of
tacks than see her straining along in a number of twists and
turns against the wind. If you sail too close there is also the
danger of "getting the boat in irons," as yachtsmen say—that
is, she has been trimmed to sail too close to the wind, and she
will not hold a definite course, but is constantly screwing into
the wind and going about first on one tack and then on the
other, all the while drifting to leeward, whilst you have to wait
helplessly watching her. In fact, she may be hung up in this
way indefinitely, until rescued by a friendly collision or line.

Watch the wind, and note if it shifts or alters in force, so
that you can adjust the trim accordingly when the yacht is put
about. Easing or tightening the jib or main sheet slightly will

make an appreciable difference. Always try to relieve a boat if her sails seem to press her unduly.

Taking down the topsail or setting a jib-headed topsail in place of a jack-yard topsail will make her ride easier in the puffs if the wind is squally. If she does not point well to windward when beating, try a smaller jib, or slacken the foresail sheet. If she regularly runs off to leeward on one tack only, whilst keeping well to windward on the other, she has some defect in construction, or perhaps a bent keel. Separate sails to suit the force of the wind are better than reefing a sail for model yachts. The accumulation of wet, bunched up canvas formed by the reefs is heavy and a drag upon the boat. A smaller sail can be set as quickly as you can reef in the larger one, and it will look and work better.

The booms of similar sails—that is, the booms of the aft-sails or the booms of the headsails—should be trimmed to approximately the same angle; that is, in a schooner, for instance, the main and spencer booms would make about the same angle with the centre line of the boat. You should not have one slackened out and the other hauled in tight; each sail on the boat ought to be doing its share of the work.

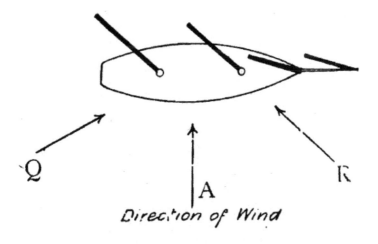

Fig. 70. A schooner reaching.

If the boat is fitted with a hatch it is a good plan to keep a sponge inside when sailing, as a small quantity of water will leak through the mast holes and hatch, and by means of the sponge this water is conveniently removed from time to time. It is a much neater method than turning your boat upside down. Spare sails and gear may be stored in the hold, but not when sailing.

Provide yourself with a repair kit, consisting of twine (that sold as "water line" is the stuff to use, and it can be obtained in several sizes), thin brass or copper wire, needle and cotton, pins, a very fine bradawl, and a pair of pliers with round points and cutting edges; also some pieces of thin cane for splicing a broken spar. Mishaps will occur, and you should be able to "repair gear" on the spot.

Do not fold up your spare sails, as they will then become creased. Spare gaff, mainssails, lugsail, and all sails fitted with a spar can be rolled up on the spar; trysails, jibs, and similar sails should be rolled up on a roller. Never leave them rolled up for any length of time when wet, but always spread them out to dry when you reach home. If any sail has been partially wetted it is a good plan to make it wet all over when sailing is finished, to prevent as far as possible the stained mark which appears, especially on the mainsail, by reason of it dipping frequently in the water to about a quarter of the way up its area. If you wet it all over whilst sailing it will become heavy. Be careful of the spars of your spare sails, especially the light topsail spars, which are very liable to be broken by accidental pressure of your hand or foot when lying on the ground. An excellent plan is to keep them on a piece of light flat wood by means of elastic bands. When sailing on a pond a light pole or stick is almost a necessity to enable the model to be comfortably turned round without getting your feet in the water. The dimensions of this pole should suit the size of boat and kind of pond; a convenient length for boats up to above 3 ft. over all would be 6 ft., and it may be, jointed for convenience in transit.

A useful accessory to have with you is a length of thin but strong cord (say, 25 yards), with a weight attached to it, such as the lead plummets used for fishing lines. This cord may be very useful to enable you to get your boat in to shore when becalmed or locked in collision with another. The way to use it is to throw the weight over the boat so that the cord engages with the rigging. You can then by steady pulling get the boat within reach; but always throw the weight clear over the boat to avoid damaging her spars.

When engaged in a race keep strictly to the sailing regulations; never do anything which may be called sharp practice. Sail for the sport, and not entirely for the prize; and always be ready to help a fellow yachtsman in distress.

Do not forget to look after your rudder, and when putting the boat out or about avoid too vigorous a use of the pole, as it may send her off the proper course. If she is coming in on a wind, place the pole under the bowsprit and bring her round stem to windward and not round to leeward. Allow the sails to fill well, and push her off gently so that she gathers speed of her own accord. Do not point her bows directly at the wind, but rather away from it, so that the wind gets into the sails; she will soon pull round if you are beating to windward.

When setting sails be careful not to strain them out of shape by too great a strain on the halyards. When setting a gaff-sail, such as the mainsail of a cutter, the tack should be fastened first, then the clew, so that the sail is evenly stretched along the boom. Then haul up the throat halyard fairly tight, and fix it; lastly, haul up the peak halyard until the sail is just free from wrinkles.

Fig. 71. Cutter beating to windward.

ON SAILING TOY-SHOP MODELS.—Though some improvements have taken place, there are still many models sold which may be rather called toys than real sailing models. They are usually found in the general toyshop or bazaar; some have hulls of a good shape, but all are usually badly fitted as regards the rigging. Many have insufficient lead on the keel, and are not very buoyant.

If the novice has come into posssession of such a model he may improve her sailing qualities by correcting the most prominent faults. If on putting the boat into water she heels over to an excessive amount, it is a sign that there is not enough lead on the keel, or that she carries too much sail. If there is a topsail fitted, take it off; if she still heels over too much, take off the foresail, if she has a jib as well. It may be advisable to dispense with a topsail altogether, and shorten the mast to relieve her as much as you can. If she has a fixed rudder the best plan is to remove it, and either sail without one or fit a self-acting swing rudder for scudding purposes. You cannot scud without one, though you may have plenty of fun reaching and beating to windward.

You will probably find that the sheets of such a boat are hauled in tight; they must be well slackened out before you try her. In many cases, if the hull seems worth it, a complete overhaul of the rigging will be an improvement. Replace all string by thin water line, and if halyards are passed through holes in the mast see that these holes are amply large, or fit small brass eyes to take their place. Lighten the boat as much as you can above the water line by removing excess length of spars, blocks of wood which may be fitted to represent cabin skylights, and similar encumbrances.

Lightning Source UK Ltd.
Milton Keynes UK
UKHW012033300920
370813UK00001B/170